# PIDAPIPÓ

# GELATO EIGHT
# DAYS A WEEK

# PIDAPIPÓ

# GELATO EIGHT
# DAYS A WEEK

WRITTEN BY

*Lisa Valmorbida*

ILLUSTRATED BY

*Jean Jullien*

hardie grant books

When I was growing up I used to daydream about owning my own restaurant. Mum had told me about a place in Melbourne where you could sit at the counter and have ice cream and milkshakes and lollies. I dreamed about owning a place like that one day, but the dream never involved me actually making the ice cream.

As I got older I became more and more obsessed with food and cooking. But working with food as a career still seemed like a dream, or something you'd do as a hobby. Maybe it was because an obsession with food was normal in my family. Lots of us cook. All of us talk obsessively about food. Dad especially trained us about food from very early on, to taste everything and to appreciate everything. I'm still obsessed with new flavours.

After high school, I enrolled in an interior design course but my focus was elsewhere. On cooking shows mainly. I'm sure my brother Jamie is exaggerating when he says I sat in the TV room watching back-to-back cooking shows for months but I do know that I spent so much time watching them that my family started to think there was something wrong with me. But these shows made it clear to me that things had to change. When I told Mum and Dad that I was dropping out of uni for a career in food their faces went white. Jamie was hovering around too. It felt like an intervention. My parents didn't exactly discourage me but they wanted to make

sure I knew what I was getting myself into. I didn't, but I told them I did because it felt like this was the right path.

I became a gelato maker gradually. Gelato had always been a part of our family life, from eating it at backyard dinners in the summer to going to Massimo's in Noosa or when we spent time in Vicenza with my Nonna and Nonno, who took us to one of the local gelaterie there. Gelato was always there. It just took me a while to notice it properly.

I completed a year-long cooking course in Sydney and landed a job at a restaurant in Melbourne called Donovans. The kitchen was equipped with a gelato machine and it fascinated me. The idea of specialising had been forming, and I wanted to focus all my energy on one thing. Jamie and I had been talking about doing a business together and one idea involved a gelato truck. I started to think gelato might be the thing.

Jamie convinced me to pursue the idea. So I researched gelato schools and the Carpigiani Gelato University in Bologna kept coming up as the best. I wasn't completely convinced that gelato was it but figured that knowing how to make authentic Italian gelato would be a great skill to have, even if the truck idea didn't go ahead. I enrolled in the course and flew to Bologna.

Italy changed everything. The Carpigiani Gelato University is at the factory where Carpigiani make their gelato machinery. Everything seemed so cool to me, like I was in exactly the right place. The course was four weeks long, taught by Italians and filled with people from all over the world.

I was immediately surprised at how calculated and specific gelato-making is. Everything is calibrated. When I cooked I didn't follow recipes, I just chucked stuff in. The challenge of having specific recipes and calibrations was what I'd been looking for.

Italy changed the way I approached gelato. Bologna is a serious foodie town where people take the idea of quality to a different level. I thought I had an understanding of what good gelato was but then I ate at La Sorbetteria Castiglione in Bologna and realised I'd never eaten good gelato before.

After finishing the course I worked at Gelateria Alberto Marchetti, one of the best gelaterias in Turin. I learned to use different machinery and was taught how to scoop gelato properly. It's a serious art form using the flat paddle. I also grew accustomed to the gelato being stored in *pozzetti* – the lidded stainless steel containers that traditional gelaterias use to hold and serve the gelato – as well as the accompanying theatre of throwing the lids around. I went to the Amalfi Coast, a prime gelato destination, and I think I went to every gelateria in the region, trying flavours and taking photos – just looking and tasting. I came home with a collection of pizza boxes, tea towels, paper bags, napkins and food wrapping as inspiration. I also had a head full of recipe ideas.

Jamie and I were still thinking of a truck but then a little shop front our family owned on Faraday Street in Carlton became available, so we decided to open a temporary store to test the concept. It was cheaper than the truck but it turned out to be one of the best ideas we had, enabling us to experiment and explore.

The name was tougher. Everything sounded stupid to me. Then my father suggested the name Pidapipó. I didn't like it at first either.

*Pidapipi* is an Italian finger game that my Nonno would play with us all whenever we were sitting around the table. It's kind of like Simon Says. You use your index finger. When you say *pidapipi*, you point up. Say *pidapipó* and you point down. The person leading the game tries to trick the players by calling out the wrong word for the gesture. If you follow the finger rather than the word, you lose. The word reminded me of Nonno and people liked the sound of it so Pidapipó it was. I can't imagine any other name now.

We opened the Pidapipó temporary store in December 2013. It was bare bones – just a neon sign, a mural painted by local artist Esther Stewart and shelves filled with ingredients as décor. We had 12 flavours at any one time and recipes for about 50 others. The

biggest expense was the gelato machinery, including the *pozzetti*. I was nervous about using them because we'd been told that people wanted to see the gelato, to look and point at the mounds in the display case. But the *pozzetti* seemed right. We were doing everything else traditionally, from using only fresh fruit, nothing frozen, to making everything on premises, and specialising solely in gelato, with no coffee, pastries or anything else, so we went for it. We were the first dedicated gelato store in Melbourne to use them, so it felt brave at the time.

We'd done some publicity and had a great launch so were expecting lines of people waiting when we opened the door. We had all these staff standing around and then ... nothing. Our first customer came in about an hour after we opened and we took a photo of her and she left. It wasn't a great start, though she did become a regular.

About seven months later we closed the temporary store ahead of opening the permanent store in Lygon Street. We celebrated by offering people a free scoop. This time, the line stretched for blocks.

When we opened the permanent Pidapipó in December 2014, we got the queue. It felt good because people knew us now. It was like being accepted as a part of the community. With the temporary store we'd started collaborating with local designers, musicians, DJs, artists, restaurateurs and producers. Music became as essential to the Pidapipó experience as the beautiful 60s-chanelling design by Rabindra Naidoo. Flavours changed all the time, the Nutella fountain flowed, we held events at restaurants and in our shop, got our own rooftop beehives, raised money for causes we cared about, threw a beach party, opened a second shop in Windsor and made a lot of gelato.

Pidapipó isn't the restaurant I daydreamed about when I was young. The dream's there though, mixed with childhood memories of gelato, my Nonno's playfulness, my experiences in Italy, a thousand hours of cooking shows, the collaboration with my brother, my family's food obsession and my fascination with the technique of gelato-making, its flavours and combinations.

I'm thrilled to be sharing these recipes and flavours that are the foundations of the Pidapipó story. I hope you become as obsessed as I am.

## Nonno Carlo

While Pidapipó was named after the game we always played with our Nonno, the reason we chose the name was to honour him – both who he was and what he accomplished.

Carlo Valmorbida emigrated to Australia from Italy in 1949 and his first job was working on a production line making Cherry Ripe chocolate bars. Six years later he and his brothers owned 14 grocery stores across Australia, including one on Lygon Street in Melbourne, the same building where we opened our first store.

Nonno was an entrepreneur and a successful businessman but he also wanted to bring Italian food and culture to Australia. We wanted to carry on his legacy at Pidapipó, which is why we make gelato the traditional Italian way – what we do is more to us than just a business.

While Nonno's first customers were from the Italian community, he believed the wider Australian community would grow to love the parmesan, tinned tuna and tomatoes, coffee, wine and mineral water that he was importing into the country. He was right.

Nonno became largely immobile after he had a stroke when I was very young and so we don't really remember what he was like before then. But he was always a very special person in our lives – hilarious, high energy, inspiring and, at times, eccentric.

He loved to shock people. He'd laugh out loud out of the blue or suddenly throw a napkin over someone's head at the dinner table or make us all line up and perform a song in our awful Italian for the whole family. And then there was *pidapipi*. It would always come from nowhere. He'd suddenly yell *pidapipi* and we'd all have to start playing and if you lost, he'd hit you with his walking stick. There was always laughter when Nonno was around.

Just before Nonno died he said to Jamie and me, 'Take your time, don't rush.' We keep that in mind with Pidapipó.

### Carob bean powder

This is used as a natural thickener, which improves the texture of the gelato by helping it absorb the water content in the recipe.

### Chocolate

When we use chocolate in our gelato-making we look to use a good-quality one with a minimum of 70 per cent cocoa solids. We get ours from local maker Huntered + Gathered, who make their chocolate in small quantities and carefully source their cocoa beans. They make a few varieties, however, we use the Dominican Republic variety for its rich, almost nutty flavour.

### Cocoa powder

We never use cocoa powder that has sugar added to it, as most of those stocked in the supermarkets do. Good-quality ones can be found at specialty food stores and include brands such as Valrhona and Callebaut.

### Cream

We use pouring (single/light) cream with a fat content of 35 per cent.

### Dextrose

Dextrose is 92 per cent as sweet as cane sugar and is used as a secondary sugar to help with a gelato's sweetness, freezing point and texture. Getting the mixture of sugars right in gelato-making is a key part of the process – for good sweetness levels, hardness and density you don't want to add more than 20–30 per cent of secondary sugars.

### Eggs

We always use free-range organic eggs, for ethical and flavour reasons (put simply, they taste better). As we don't use egg as an emulsifier in our gelato, it's only used when we want to taste it, therefore it's important that the eggs we use are the freshest and best quality we can lay our hands on.

### Hazelnut and pistachio pastes

I prefer to use nut pastes in my gelatos over grinding the nuts myself because the industrial machines used are able to grind them finely enough to extract all the oils and flavours and ensure you don't get a grainy texture, resulting in a better product than I can make myself. Nut pastes can be hard to find, so I suggest ordering them online or try specialty food stores – look for varieties that are 100 per cent hazelnut or pistachio nut and preferably from the Piedmont (for hazelnuts) or Bronte (for pistachio nuts) regions of Italy, as these nuts have the best flavour. If you want to add extra nutty texture to your gelatos, you can add roasted crushed nuts to the final product.

### Milk

We use full-cream homogenised jersey milk when making gelato because of its high protein levels – higher than other types of milk – as these proteins help to trap air during the gelato-making process, ensuring the gelato doesn't shrink and making it as creamy as possible. It's important that the milk is homogenised because you want the particles to be fully broken down so the water content can be absorbed properly when adding the other ingredients. We also prefer that the milk is organic with a fat content of 3.5 per cent. If you can't find jersey milk, ordinary full-cream milk is fine too.

### Vanilla paste

We use good-quality vanilla paste and suggest you do the same. Check the label when purchasing to make sure that your vanilla paste is pure and not made from any synthetic ingredients.

### Water

We prefer filtered, pure, still water to make our gelatos, but if you're happy drinking your tap water then you can, of course, use this.

### Gelato/ice cream machine

Gelato and ice cream machines come in all shapes, sizes and types, but for our purposes we recommend using those machines that have the freezing compartment built in. Your aim when making gelato is to freeze the mixture as fast as possible to lessen the ice crystals. Those machines that lack a freezing compartment – where the canister is frozen before use – take at least twice as long to freeze the gelato and will leave you with an icier product. As a general rule of thumb, the more you spend on a machine, the better your end product will be. In the store I use a commercial Carpigiani machine, one of the best brands. While they do make a countertop machine, it's very expensive – I trialled all my recipes for this book using a regular Cuisinart gelato maker and the results were fine.

### Gelato scoops

Metal scoopers are always best and I often dip them in hot water before using them to get a perfectly smooth ball. We use flat pallet scoopers in store, however these require a bit of getting used to, so aren't recommended unless you are planning on putting in the time to master this skill!

### Metal trays

We use metal trays to make our granitas because they get colder quicker, giving you a perfect icy product with the right consistency.

### Scales

As you need to be exact when measuring ingredients for gelato recipes – particularly small quantities of thickeners and emulsifiers such as carob bean powder and guar gum – it is important to use an accurate electronic scale. Gelato recipes are all about getting the balance right between the fats, sugars and solid ingredients added, and if you're not exact you can throw off the whole recipe and end up with a different product. This is why all the ingredients in our recipes are measured in grams rather than millilitres or cups.

### Serving note

You can eat your gelato soft, straight from the machine or, if you prefer a firmer gelato, it will need longer in the freezer and may need to be left out to soften a little before serving. The temperature of your freezer will determine the length of time that you need to leave the gelato out – the perfect serving temperature is about −8°C (18°F). The warmer you serve your gelato, the more flavour you will have – this is a big reason we use the *pozzetti* system in store because it allows you to serve your gelato at a warmer temperature.

18

SPRING

# 55

PRIMAVERA

I like spring at Pidapipó because you can see customers getting excited as new flavours start to appear on the menu. Strawberries arrive, then apricots and limes and so on. Some regulars greet them like old friends.

All the fruit we use for gelato in the shop we store and prepare in the open so that it becomes part of the décor. It's a good way to mark the changing of the seasons. I like the idea because it literally shows that we're open about our ingredients and not using frozen or pre-made sauces and mixes, and that we're following the traditions of the best gelato makers in Italy.

Having all our ingredients and machinery as part of the décor was really important to us when we were planning the design of the permanent shop. We wanted it to feel authentically Italian, classic and timeless rather than trendy. It was about the small details – using materials that are constant and classic like marble, concrete and wood – and getting an Italian feel with a design that improves with age.

Design is one of the things that Jamie and I work on together at Pidapipó. With some of the business, we just trust each other to get on with things. He's good at some things; I'm good at others. He doesn't read the recipes that I create and I let him take care of the marketing and business side of things. We've always been clear about what we're both doing; we trust each other. For me that's the best kind of business and why Pidapipó has worked.

With the design of the permanent shop we put together a list of what we wanted, sketched out a plan of where we thought things might go and then started to shop around for a designer we could work with. We really liked the work of Rabindra Naidoo. He was a bit hard to track down but when we did finally meet him, we immediately knew he was the right person. He understood what we were talking about and very quickly drew up the plans, which was good as it was spring already and our planned early summer opening date was rapidly approaching.

It was funny that I instantly liked what Rabindra showed us because I'd initially talked to him about a more colourful shop and then he came back with this quite minimal concrete and white idea that was not at all what I'd imagined. But I saw he had really understood the brief. The pared-back look with all the small details really captured what we were after. It also reminded me of when I was younger and had been daydreaming of owning restaurants. One of those daydreams had been about an all-white restaurant, so maybe I did get what I wanted.

Spring is always a time when we throw a few parties, get DJs or musicians into the shop to play and maybe launch a new flavour or a new range.

Music has always been an important part of Pidapipó. Well, almost always. Our approach to music, having DJs play live or getting them to create playlists for the shop came about really early on with the temporary store and it happened through a combination of intuition and some really bad techno.

Jamie had a conversation with a successful restaurateur about the shop who suggested that, to attract the attention of the crowd, what we needed was some full-on techno, no vocals, turned up really loud. So Jamie brought a techno playlist in, turned it up and then just walked out and left me in there. No one came in and it was a really awful atmosphere so I ended up turning it right down so that you could hardly hear it. People started to come in again. That was when I realised we needed to get music that suited us. I contacted a friend of ours who's a DJ and asked him to make me a playlist. He brought it in, we stuck it on and the atmosphere of the place changed completely. People would stick around to listen to the music. Now we're always updating the music in our stores and working with the best people in Melbourne who can help us get the best atmosphere. It's really helped define the personality of Pidapipó and is an important part of the whole experience. It was one of those things we discovered through doing the temporary store.

The temporary store was like Pidapipó's spring. We learned so much from it that we were able to use in the permanent store: what people liked in terms of product, the layout of the store and how customers use it, the music, bringing the ice cream machine to the front window and chopping fruit in the store so the process of the gelato being made becomes part of the experience.

Our first collaborations also started at the temporary store. There was the Esther Stewart mural and the uniforms designed by a Melbourne-based fashion label called PAM, but we also worked with some of the local traders, including a pizza joint called DOC.

We've since done a few collaborations with Tony Nicolini, who owns DOC. He comes to me with specific requests, like making a fior di latte with buffalo milk or doing a sesame gelato for a dish he was thinking about that he wanted to be all black. But the thing we've done most with him are collaborations with dessert pizza. We held one of these in the back courtyard of DOC where we were selling sweet pizzas to the public that were all pared with a different gelato. We had a strawberry pizza teamed with fior di latte, banana with macadamia and coconut gelato and another that was like a cassata with nuts and ricotta.

Spring is always a time of new ideas. It's a season that really suits Pidapipó.

**Lemon sorbetto**
*Sorbetto al limone*

**Makes 1 kg (2 lb 3 oz/10 scoops)**

**Ingredients:**
**200 g (7 oz) lemon juice**
**500 g (1 lb 2 oz) filtered water**
**5 g (¼ oz) carob bean powder**
**280 g (10 oz) caster (superfine) sugar**

*Lemon sorbetto is one of the few fruity gelato or sorbetto recipes where you don't want the fruit to be overripe. With this one, you want the lemons to be as fresh and as tart as possible, rather than too ripe and too sweet. Also, when you're juicing them, be careful to avoid including any pith as this can make the sorbet bitter.*

1   Put the lemon juice and water in a bowl and whiz briefly with a hand-held blender to combine.

2   Put the carob bean powder in a separate bowl. Add 2 tablespoons of the sugar and mix together well.

3   Gradually add the carob powder and sugar mixture to the lemon juice mixture, blending all the while, until well combined. Add the rest of the sugar and blend to incorporate, then transfer to a suitable lidded container and leave to cool in the freezer for 15–20 minutes, or until the mixture drops to 4°C (39°F).

4   Turn on your gelato maker so it begins the freezing process.

5   Pour the mixture into your gelato maker. Once the mixture reaches –4°C (25°F) (this should take about 30–40 minutes) detach the canister or scoop the sorbetto into a pre-cooled lidded container. Transfer to the freezer and leave for at least 1 hour to harden before serving.

Spring
*Primavera*

**Milk gelato**
*Gelato al fior di latte*

Makes 1 kg (2 lb 3 oz/10 scoops)

Ingredients:
135 g (5 oz) caster (superfine) sugar
35 g (1¼ oz) dextrose
20 g (¾ oz) skim milk powder
5 g (¼ oz) carob bean powder
645 g (1 lb 7 oz) milk
165 ml (5½ fl oz) pouring (single/light)
      cream

*This is the Italian version of vanilla ice cream and is what all the kids eat in Italy, a sort of entry-level gelato. It's really plain, just made with milk with no vanilla or any other flavour added. I actually prefer this to vanilla ice cream because the flavour is just so clean.*

1    Put the sugar, dextrose and skim milk powder in a bowl and mix to combine.

2    Put the carob bean powder in a separate bowl. Add 2 tablespoons of the sugar mixture and mix together well.

3    Pour the milk and cream into a large heavy-based saucepan over a medium heat. Whisk in the carob bean powder mixture and continue to heat, whisking in the sugar mixture as you go, until it hits 85°C (185°F). Remove from the heat, pour into a suitable lidded container and leave to cool in the freezer for 1 hour, or until the mixture drops to 4°C (39°F).

4    Turn on your gelato maker so it begins the freezing process.

5    Pour the mixture into your gelato maker. Once the mixture reaches –4°C (25°F) or is the consistency of soft-serve ice cream (this should take about 30–45 minutes) detach the canister or scoop the gelato into a pre-cooled lidded container. Transfer to the freezer and leave for at least 1 hour to harden before serving.

**Chocolate gelato**
*Gelato al cioccolato*

**Makes 1 kg (2 lb 3 oz/10 scoops)**

**Ingredients:**
95 g (3¼ oz) caster (superfine) sugar
55 g (2 oz) dextrose
15 g (½ oz) skim milk powder
40 g (1½ oz) dark muscovado sugar
55 g (2 oz) Dutch (unsweetened) cocoa
    powder
3 g (1/8 oz) carob bean powder
460 g (1 lb) milk
115 ml (4 fl oz) pouring (single/light)
    cream
155 g (5½ oz) filtered water
50 g (1¾ oz) dark chocolate (70% cocoa
    solids), broken into small chunks

*This recipe was the hardest to get right and took me the longest of any of the flavours. I made so much chocolate gelato to get to this one it was crazy. My mum was the tester and she's really tough so I was happy when she finally approved this one. The biggest secret? Make sure to use the best chocolate you can find, never just cocoa powder. We use chocolate from Hunted + Gathered. They make the chocolate from scratch, from the beans, and use no dairy. I've never tasted chocolate as good as theirs. It's strong, intense and not sweet, meaning you can really taste the bean.*

1   Put the caster sugar, dextrose, skim milk powder, dark muscovado sugar and cocoa powder in a bowl and mix to combine.

2   Put the carob bean powder in a separate bowl. Add 2 tablespoons of the sugar mixture and mix together well.

3   Pour the milk, cream and water into a large heavy-based saucepan over a medium heat. Whisk in the carob bean powder mixture and continue to heat, whisking in the sugar mixture as you go, until it hits 85°C (185°F). Remove from the heat, add the chocolate and whisk together until the chocolate has melted into the mixture and everything is well combined. Pour into a suitable lidded container and leave to cool in the freezer for 1 hour, or until the mixture drops to 4°C (39°F).

4   Turn on your gelato maker so it begins the freezing process.

5   Pour the mixture into your gelato maker. Once the mixture reaches –4°C (25°F) or is the consistency of soft-serve ice cream (this should take about 30–45 minutes) detach the canister or scoop the gelato into a pre-cooled lidded container. Transfer to the freezer and leave for at least 1 hour to harden before serving.

**Banoffee pie**
*Torta banoffee*

**Serves 8**

**Ingredients:**
190 g (6½ oz) digestive biscuits
    (graham crackers)
110 g (4 oz) unsalted butter
110 g (4 oz) dark chocolate (70% cocoa
    solids), plus extra for shaving
1 kg (2 lb 3 oz/10 scoops) Banana milk
    gelato (page 38)
500 ml (17 fl oz/2 cups) pouring
    (single/light) cream
50 g (1¾ oz) icing (confectioners') sugar
3 g (1/8 oz) vanilla paste
1 ripe banana, sliced
8 maraschino cherries

**Banana caramel sauce**
100 g (3½ oz) very ripe banana, chopped
155 g (5½ oz) soft brown sugar
160 ml (5½ fl oz) pouring (single/light)
    cream
50 g (1¾ oz) unsalted butter

*When I was trying to come up with cakes for the shop, I didn't want to go down the usual path of layered ice cream cakes with funny decorations on the top so I started to think about regular desserts that might translate well as gelato cakes. Bombe Alaska was an obvious one and then I started thinking of pies because the shell would work when it's frozen and can be filled with whatever flavours you like. Banoffee pie is one of those desserts that had fallen out of fashion for years but suddenly started popping up in cafes all over town, so it seemed like the right time to give it the gelato treatment.*

1    To make the banana caramel sauce, add the banana, sugar and cream to a heavy-based saucepan over a medium–high heat and heat for 1–2 minutes until bubbling. Remove from the heat and blend with a hand-held blender until smooth, then whisk in the butter until incorporated. Pour into a bowl and transfer to the fridge to chill.

2    Place the biscuits in a large bowl and crush them with the end of a rolling pin to a fine crumb (alternatively, blitz them briefly to a similar consistency in a food processor).

3    Melt the butter and chocolate together in a double boiler set over a medium–high heat. Pour the mixture over the crushed biscuits and stir to combine.

4    Spoon the biscuit crumb mixture into a 20 cm (8 in) loose-bottomed pie tin and press it into the base to cover evenly, being sure to leave no gaps. Spoon over the banana gelato and spread it with a palette knife to form an even layer, then transfer to the freezer and leave to chill for 1 hour.

5    Remove the pie from the freezer and pour over the banana caramel sauce evenly, then return to the freezer for a further 1 hour, or until ready to serve.

6    When ready to serve, whisk the cream, icing sugar and vanilla paste together in a mixing bowl to form soft peaks. Arrange half the banana slices over the caramel in an even layer, dollop over the whipped vanilla cream, then top with the maraschino cherries and remaining banana slices and shave a little extra dark chocolate over the top to finish.

**Avocado and lime sorbetto**
*Sorbetto all'avocado e lime*

**Makes 1 kg (2 lb 3 oz/10 scoops)**

**Ingredients:**
**300 g (10½ oz) avocado flesh**
**100 g (3½ oz) freshly squeezed lime juice**
**360 g (12½ oz) filtered water**
**5 g (¼ oz) carob bean powder**
**200 g (7 oz) caster (superfine) sugar**

*I normally just like traditional flavours, so avocado and lime is about as weird as I get. It came about when I was making smoothies for breakfast and experimenting with different flavours. One day I tried avocado and lime and the texture the avocado gave the smoothie was lovely and creamy and the lime lifted it with its acidity. I'd always wanted to make a citrus sorbet with a creamy texture and the smoothie showed me how to achieve that. This is now one of my favourite flavours.*

1    Put the avocado flesh, lime juice and water in a bowl and blend with a hand-held blender until smooth.

2    Put the carob bean powder in a separate bowl. Add 2 tablespoons of the sugar and mix together well.

3    Gradually add the carob powder and sugar mixture to the avocado mixture, blending all the while, until well combined. Add the rest of the sugar and blend to incorporate, then transfer to a suitable lidded container and leave to cool in the freezer for 15–20 minutes, or until the mixture drops to 4°C (39°F).

4    Turn on your gelato maker so it begins the freezing process.

5    Pour the mixture into your gelato maker. Once the mixture reaches –4°C (25°F) (this should take about 30–40 minutes) detach the canister or scoop the sorbetto into a pre-cooled lidded container. Transfer to the freezer and leave for at least 1 hour to harden before serving.

**Piña colada sorbetto**
*Sorbetto alla Piña colada*

**Makes 1 kg (2 lb 3 oz/10 scoops)**

**Ingredients:**
**500 g (1 lb 2 oz) pineapple, cored and
    chopped**
**260 g (9 oz) coconut milk**
**5 g (¼ oz) carob bean powder**
**160 g (5½ oz) caster (superfine) sugar**
**75 g (2¾ oz) dextrose**

*Nothing reminds me more of hot, sunny days than the flavours of a piña
colada. Although the acidity of the pineapples here helps keep things really
refreshing, the coconut milk used in place of water makes this denser
and richer than a typical sorbetto. It's great for vegans searching for that
richness that dairy products lend desserts, and works well as a substitute
for water in sorbetto recipes across the board – I particularly like it with
mango or lemon.*

1   Put the pineapple and coconut milk in a bowl and blend with
    a hand-held blender until smooth.

2   Put the carob bean powder in a separate bowl. Add
    2 tablespoons of the sugar and mix together well.

3   Gradually add the carob powder and sugar mixture to the
    pineapple mixture, blending all the while, until well combined.
    Add the rest of the sugar and the dextrose and blend to
    incorporate, then transfer to a suitable lidded container and
    leave to cool in the freezer for 15–20 minutes, or until the
    mixture drops to 4°C (39°F).

4   Turn on your gelato maker so it begins the freezing process.

5   Pour the mixture into your gelato maker. Once the mixture
    reaches –4°C (25°F) (this should take about 30–45 minutes)
    detach the canister or scoop the sorbetto into a pre-cooled
    lidded container. Transfer to the freezer and leave for at least
    1 hour to harden before serving.

**Makes 5 popsicles**

**Ingredients:**

480 g (1 lb 1 oz) (enough to fill 5 moulds)
    Salted caramel gelato (page 50)
100 g (3½ oz) milk chocolate, broken
    into small chunks
40 g (1½ oz) cocoa butter

**Malt crumble**
140 g (5 oz) unsalted butter, melted
85 g (3 oz) malt powder
175 g (6 oz) plain (all-purpose) flour
100 g (3½ oz) caster (superfine) sugar

**Salted caramel, milk choc and malt crumble popsicle**
*Ghiacciolo al caramello salato, cioccolato al latte e briciolata di mandorle*

*This is a take on the classic Australian ice cream, the Golden Gaytime. It starts with salted caramel gelato dipped in milk chocolate that's then rolled in a malt crumble. These are really sweet but they're always a hit when you serve them at parties.*

1   Preheat the oven to 170°C (340°F/Gas 3). Line two baking trays with non-stick baking paper.

2   To make the malt crumble, put all the ingredients in a bowl and mix together with your hands to form a crumble-like mixture. Arrange on one of the prepared baking trays in an even layer and cook for 20 minutes until lightly golden, breaking the crumble up with a fork and mixing it around halfway through cooking. Remove from the oven and leave to cool, then break into breadcrumb-sized pieces with your hands. Set aside.

3   Fill five 60 ml (2 fl oz/¼ cup) popsicle moulds with the salted caramel gelato and push a popsicle stick halfway down in the centre of each. Transfer to the freezer and leave to harden for 4 hours.

4   Once the gelato has hardened, briefly place one of the moulds popsicle stick–side up (being sure that no water touches the gelato) in a jug of warm water. Remove the mould from the water, turn it upside down and pull gently on the popsicle stick until the popsicle comes out, then transfer to the tray lined with non-stick baking paper. Repeat with the remaining moulds, then return the popsicles to the freezer and leave for a further 2 hours to harden.

5   Melt the milk chocolate and cocoa butter together in a double boiler or a bowl in the microwave, then pour into a tall container and leave to cool slightly. Dip a popsicle into the chocolate, then transfer it to the tray with the malted crumbs and turn to coat each side (you need to do this quickly before the chocolate solidifies). Repeat with the remaining popsicles. Eat straight away or place the popsicles back on the lined tray and return to the freezer until needed.

TOMOBILISTICA ITALIANA

—

CENZA SOCIALE

557

lida per la partecipazione
Soci dell' A. C. I. alle ma-
estazioni chiuse e sociali)

sciata per l'anno 1949

Sig. Valmorbida Carlo

eudonimo autorizzato Pozzo valdu

cio effettivo dell'A. C. di Vicenza

o a Villaganzerla (Vicenza

miciliato a Castegnero

Data 23.1.1948

IL PRESIDENTE

Timbro

Caramelised banana split
*Banana split caramellata*

Serves 4

Ingredients:

100 ml (3½ fl oz) pouring (single/light)
    cream
1½ tablespoons icing (confectioners')
    sugar, plus extra if necessary
2 ripe bananas
200 g (7 oz/2 scoops) Chocolate gelato
    (page 32)
200 g (7 oz/2 scoops) Milk gelato
    (page 30)
200 g (7 oz/2 scoops) Salted caramel
    gelato (page 50)
8 amarena cherries

Peanut croccante

2 tablespoons glucose syrup
135 g (5 oz) caster (superfine) sugar
135 g (5 oz) roasted peanuts

Chocolate fudge sauce

250 ml (8½ fl oz/1 cup) pouring (single/
    light) cream
100 g (3½ oz) soft brown sugar
2 tablespoons golden syrup or maple
    syrup
20 g (¾ oz) unsalted butter
200 g (7 oz) dark chocolate (70% cocoa
    solids), broken into chunks

*This is a classic banana split, tweaked. I had to include it because when I was growing up it was one of my favourite things in the world. Me and my best friend would always make banana splits when we were kids but this one is a little more adult than that, with a bit more technique involved. It's still a banana split at heart, though.*

1   For the peanut croccante, add the glucose syrup and caster sugar to a small saucepan over a high heat. Cook, stirring, until caramelised and very dark brown in colour, then add the peanuts and mix together thoroughly. Carefully tip the mixture out onto the centre of a heatproof silicone mat, cover with non-stick baking paper and roll out with a rolling pin as thin as possible. Leave to cool, then pull off the paper and chop into small pieces. Set aside until needed (this will keep for months in an airtight container).

2   To make the chocolate fudge sauce, add the cream, sugar, golden syrup and butter to a heavy-based saucepan and stir to combine. Bring to a simmer, then remove from the heat, add the chocolate and whisk together until the chocolate has melted into the mixture and everything is well combined. Keep warm over a low heat.

3   Whip the cream and 2 teaspoons of the icing sugar together in a bowl to form soft peaks. Set aside.

4   Slice the bananas lengthways in half and place cut-side up on a baking tray.

5   Sprinkle the remaining icing sugar over the bananas to cover completely (adding a little more if you need) and caramelise with a blowtorch or place under a hot grill for a few minutes until nicely golden.

6   To serve, arrange the caramelised banana slices side-by-side on a serving plate. Place a scoop of each gelato next to one another in the centre of each banana and dollop over the cream. Pour over the fudge sauce (or alternatively serve this on the side) and top with the croccante and amarena cherries.

Salted caramel gelato
*Gelato al caramello salato*

**Makes 1 kg (2 lb 3 oz/10 scoops)**

**Ingredients:**
135 g (5 oz) caster (superfine) sugar
150 g (5½ oz) filtered water
645 g (1 lb 7 oz) milk
165 ml (5½ fl oz) pouring (single/light)
    cream
35 g (1¼ oz) dextrose
20 g (¾ oz) skim milk powder
5 g (¼ oz) carob bean powder
7 g (¼ oz) sea salt

*I don't get salted caramel gelato myself. It's too sweet for me but I have included it here because it's our most popular flavour at both our shops – we sell almost triple the amount of it compared to any other flavour. People love it on its own but it makes more sense to me when it's teamed with something else.*

1    Put the sugar in a heavy-based saucepan and stir in the water to make a slurry. Put the pan on the stove top over a medium–high heat and leave for 3 minutes to caramelise (don't stir it during this time, just leave it to do its thing). When the caramel is a nice dark brown, remove the pan from the stove and whisk in the milk and then the cream.

2    Put all the remaining ingredients in a bowl and mix to combine.

3    Return the pan to the heat and gradually whisk in the combined ingredients until fully incorporated. Continue to heat, whisking as you go, until it hits 85°C (185°F). Remove from the heat, pour into a suitable lidded container and leave to cool in the freezer for 1 hour, or until the mixture drops to 4°C (39°F).

4    Turn on your gelato maker so it begins the freezing process.

5    Pour the mixture into your gelato maker. Once the mixture reaches –4°C (25°F) or is the consistency of soft-serve ice cream (this should take about 30–45 minutes) detach the canister or scoop the gelato into a pre-cooled lidded container. Transfer to the freezer and leave for at least 1 hour to harden before serving.

## Banana milk gelato
### *Gelato al latte di banana*

**Makes 1 kg (2 lb 3 oz/10 scoops)**

Ingredients:
**160 g (5½ oz) caster (superfine) sugar**
**35 g (1¼ oz) dextrose**
**20 g (¾ oz) skim milk powder**
**5 g (¼ oz) carob bean powder**
**645 g (1 lb 7 oz) milk**
**165 ml (5½ fl oz) pouring (single/light)**
    **cream**
**80 g (2¾ oz) over-ripe banana, chopped**

*This is the gelato that I use in our Banoffee pie (page 38). Our customers at Pidapipó are always pleased when we have it on the menu because it can be hard to come by, especially when made with real bananas like this (often the places that do have it use fake flavouring so that it has a bright yellow colour). We never have the bananas we use in our gelato on display because you have to leave them until they're completely black and disgusting. We store them out the back and try to hide them as we're using them – they look foul but the taste is amazing and makes this one of our most popular flavours.*

1    Put the sugar, dextrose and skim milk powder in a bowl and mix to combine.

2    Put the carob bean powder in a separate bowl. Add 2 tablespoons of the sugar mixture and mix together well.

3    Pour the milk and cream into a large heavy-based saucepan over a medium heat. Whisk in the carob bean powder mixture and continue to heat, whisking in the sugar mixture as you go, until it hits 85°C (185°F). Remove from the heat, pour into a suitable lidded container and leave to cool in the freezer for 1 hour, or until the mixture drops to 4°C (39°F).

4    Turn on your gelato maker so it begins the freezing process.

5    Add the banana to the mixture and blend with a hand-held blender until very smooth.

6    Pour the mixture into your gelato maker. Once the mixture reaches −4°C (25°F) or is the consistency of soft-serve ice cream (this should take about 30–45 minutes) detach the canister or scoop the gelato into a pre-cooled lidded container. Transfer to the freezer and leave for at least 1 hour to harden before serving.

**TIP** Make sure the bananas you use here are completely black; they will be gooey and very soft but will give you an amazing, strong banana flavour.

Spring
*Primavera*

**Chocolate and peanut butter parfait layer cake with salted caramel sauce**
*Semifreddo al ciocciolato e burro d'arachidi con crema di caramello salato*

Serves 10

Ingredients:

**Peanut butter parfait**
100 ml (3½ fl oz) pouring (single/light) cream
10 g (⅛ oz) icing (confectioners') sugar
500 g (1 lb 2 oz/5 scoops) Peanut butter and chocolate fudge gelato (page 127)

**Chocolate parfait**
300 ml (10 fl oz) pouring (single/light) cream
30 g (¼ oz) icing (confectioners') sugar
600 g (1 lb 5 oz/6 scoops) Chocolate gelato (page 32)

**Salted caramel sauce**
155 g (5½ oz) soft brown sugar
160 ml (5½ fl oz) pouring (single/light) cream
50 g (1¾ oz) unsalted butter
2 teaspoons sea salt

*Gelato is always best when it's eaten fresh – every day it sits in the freezer it loses some integrity. This is why in Italy the gelaterias make cakes with what's left over at the end of the day. They mix the left-over gelato with cream and whip it to freshen it up. This recipe is based on those cakes and, as such, can be made successfully with pretty much any leftover flavour that you happen to have left in the freezer, so feel free to try experimenting here.*

1 Line a 25 x 11 cm (10 x 4¼ in) square cake tin with plastic wrap and put it in the freezer along with the bowl of an electric mixer to chill for 10 minutes.

2 For the peanut butter parfait, add the cream and icing sugar to the chilled bowl of the electric mixer with the whisk attachment added and beat together to form soft peaks. Switch to the paddle attachment, add the gelato and beat until combined, then spoon the mixture into the prepared cake tin and gently spread it with a palette knife to form an even layer. Transfer to the freezer and leave for 1 hour to harden slightly.

3 Clean the mixer bowl and return to the freezer to chill for at least 10 minutes.

4 For the chocolate parfait, add the cream and icing sugar to the bowl of the electric mixer with the whisk attachment added and beat together to form soft peaks. Switch to the paddle attachment, add the gelato and beat until combined, then spoon the mixture over the peanut butter parfait and gently spread it with a palette knife to form an even layer. Transfer to the freezer and leave for 2 hours to harden.

5 Meanwhile, to make the salted caramel sauce, add the brown sugar and cream to a small heavy-based saucepan over a medium heat, whisk to combine and bring to the boil. Add the butter and cook, whisking continuously, until it has melted completely. Add the sea salt and whisk to combine, then transfer to the fridge to chill.

6 When ready to serve, pull on the edges of the plastic wrap to remove the parfait from the mould and cut into slices. Spoon a little of the caramel sauce over the centre of individual serving plates and top each with a cake slice. Serve.

56

I always get excited at the start of every season because of the different ingredients that become available. It's not that you get sick of the ones you've been using but it's sometimes easy to forget about some ingredients until the seasons change and they're suddenly back again. It's exciting. But I get extra excited when summer arrives, not just because warm weather, summer nights and gelato go so well together but also because of the amazing variety of ingredients you get to work with.

Summer to me has always been about fruit. Both my mother and father are great cooks and love to entertain and so summer reminds me of the dinners we would have in our backyard that would include lots of fresh fruit: mangoes, strawberries, rockmelon, pineapple, watermelon, plums, peaches, passionfruit and cherries. These are some of the flavours I return to when I think about making gelato and sorbet in summer.

It was summer when I learned about how important it is to use really good-quality fresh fruit when you're making gelato. I was enrolled at the Carpigiani Gelato University and it was July, summer in Bologna, and really, really hot. It was also the time of year when some of the best-quality fruit is available. In Italy, the quality of fruit is like a different standard altogether. When you eat a peach in Bologna in summer it's like you've never really eaten a peach before. The intensity of the flavour, the juiciness.

It sets a high standard but it also made me understand that I couldn't compromise: you can't make good gelato without using great ingredients.

One of the first things they emphasised at Carpigiani was to always use fresh fruit, never frozen. But you also need to learn when to use the fruit. A piece of fruit that's perfect for biting into has a different degree of ripeness altogether to the fruit you use when you're making gelato. To get the kind of concentrated flavour you need for gelato, you have to do some extreme ripening. I get bananas in when they're green and don't use them until they've turned black, for example, while strawberries I leave until they're soft and collapsing in on themselves. It concentrates the sugar and makes the flavour more intense. It's why when people come into Pidapipó and try our fruit-flavoured gelato they often comment on how much it tastes like fresh fruit. It's because that's what it's flavoured with. We don't hide behind anything else. It's also what makes our gelato seasonal. You're not going to get mango gelato in winter at Pidapipó.

Both the Pidapipó temporary store and the permanent store in Lygon Street opened in summer. It was a matter of timing and practicality but it was also a business move too. Gelato is still considered a bit of a seasonal thing in Australia, something that people mainly eat when the weather is warm. It's easier to get

people's attention in summer and I think we'll always be busiest when it's warm but, after spending time in Italy where gelato is more of a year-round thing, I think it could easily change here too.

Summer is the time when Pidapipó throws some of its best parties. Jamie and I always like to collaborate with a variety of different people – it kind of pushes you to do things that you may not have thought about on your own.

We did a collaboration for Valentine's Day with a local design studio called Tin & Ed. Every year we do a flavour for the night and have a DJ playing in the store and initially we approached Tin & Ed to do something in the window of the shop so people would know what we were doing and what the flavour was. Then we decided that we would collaborate on the actual gelato too. The concept was 'when opposites attract' and their approach was really visual, they just wanted a really good colour. My brief was to come up with some kind of salty-sweet flavour that was not too obvious but also not weird enough that people wouldn't want to eat it. We did a blackberry and salted chocolate that was this amazing bright purple-mauve colour with a strange but exciting taste. People still ask for it.

For the St Kilda Festival one year we decided that we'd do an Italian kind of thing and hold a beach, bocce and gelato party. We set up on part of St Kilda beach and laid out two bocce courts and set up a gelato stand. We also had DJs playing all day. It was a perfect beach day, hot and sunny, and it was pretty tame for most of the day but as the evening came, more and more people started to turn up and we ended up having this massive beach party with people dancing. Jamie and I looked at each other at one stage, going 'what is happening here?' It was an amazing night. And we sold a lot of gelato.

Just after we opened the permanent shop we threw a party around Christmas time to launch a new flavour that I'd been working on since that spring. The gelato was based on banoffee pie, a classic English toffee and banana dessert, but I also created it in collaboration with an amazing Melbourne musician, Martha Brown, who plays under the name Banoffee. For the launch she played in the laneway next to the shop. It was like our own mini music festival.

I'm always sorry to see summer go. But just like the many great ingredients that are ripe and available at the same time, it will be back.

Summer
*Estaté*

**Makes 1 kg (2 lb 3 oz/10 scoops)**

**Ingredients:**
**600 g (1 lb 5 oz) very ripe strawberries,
    hulled**
**220 g (8 oz) filtered water**
**5 g (¼ oz) carob bean powder**
**270 g (9½ oz) caster (superfine) sugar**

*I always use fresh strawberries, never frozen, because the flavour is more real. Frozen fruit might give you a more consistent flavour but with fresh fruit, the flavour's always changing slightly and I love that – it becomes all about the seasons. You need to ripen the strawberries until they're at that dark squishy stage. It concentrates all the sugar. They look a bit weird and you wouldn't want to eat them like that but the flavour is amazing.*

1    Put the strawberries and water in a bowl and blend with a hand-held blender until smooth.

2    Put the carob bean powder in a separate bowl. Add 2 tablespoons of the sugar and mix together well.

3    Gradually add the carob powder and sugar mixture to the strawberry mixture, blending all the while, until well combined. Add the rest of the sugar and blend to incorporate, then transfer to a suitable lidded container and leave to cool in the freezer for 15–20 minutes, or until the mixture drops to 4°C (39°F).

4    Turn on your gelato maker so it begins the freezing process.

5    Pour the mixture into your gelato maker. Once the mixture reaches –4°C (25°F) (this should take about 30–60 minutes) detach the canister or scoop the sorbetto into a pre-cooled lidded container. Transfer to the freezer and leave for at least 1 hour to harden before serving.

## Watermelon and mint granita
### *Granita all'anguria e menta*

**Serves 4**

**Ingredients:**
**500 g (1 lb 2 oz) seedless watermelon,**
**cut into small chunks**
**300 g (10½ oz) filtered water**
**10 large mint leaves**
**200 g (7 oz) caster (superfine) sugar**

*Watermelon always reminds me of summer. My mother never liked it – which I always found weird – but she made sure it was always there in the fridge in summer. Watermelon is a classic granita flavour in Italy, and the watermelon/mint/ice combination here is very refreshing and perfect on its own, though if you want to get more adult, try forking some vodka or prosecco through it before serving. It's important to pay attention while making granita to make sure you get the right slushy consistency. And eat it straight away – if you leave it in the freezer it'll go rock hard.*

1   Add the watermelon, water, mint and sugar to a bowl and blend with a hand-held blender until completely smooth.

2   Pour the mixture into a pre-cooled stainless steel tray and put into the freezer. Every 30 minutes, remove and break up the ice crystals with a fork. Do this until icy and easy to scoop (this should take about 2 hours). Serve.

**Rockmelon granita with whipped cream**
*Granita al melone con panna montata*

**Serves 4**

**Ingredients:**
500 g (1 lb 2 oz) rockmelon (netted melon/
cantaloupe), cut into small chunks
300 g (10½ oz) filtered water
200 g (7 oz) raw (demerara) sugar

**Whipped cream**
200 ml (7 fl oz) pouring (single/light)
cream
20 g (¾ oz) icing (confectioners')
sugar, sifted

*The first time I had a granita with cream was in Italy. They put this really thick cream on top of the granita and then you eat it together. It's such a good combination, really creamy, almost like a Weiss bar. Rockmelon is really good in granita. It's a dense kind of fruit and the texture makes the granita less icy.*

1    Add the rockmelon, water and raw sugar to a bowl and blend with a hand-held blender until completely smooth.

2    Pour the mixture into a pre-cooled stainless steel tray and put into the freezer. Every 30 minutes, remove and break up the ice crystals with a fork. Do this until icy and easy to scoop (this should take about 2 hours).

3    Add the cream and sifted icing sugar to a cold mixing bowl and whisk to form hard peaks.

4    Spoon the granita into glasses and top each with a dollop of the whipped cream. Serve with spoons and straws.

# Raspberry and rose bombe alaska
## *Bombe alaska ai lamponi e rose*

*We offer two versions of bombe alaska at Pidapipó, this one with raspberry and rose gelato and then another version made with bacio gelato (page 122). This one is lighter and better suited to summer, when the berries are at their best.*

**Serves 4**

**Ingredients:**
305 g (11 oz) Raspberry and rose gelato (page 75)

**Chocolate cake**
175 g (6 oz) unsalted butter, cubed
225 g (8 oz) dark chocolate (70% cocoa solids), broken into small chunks
6 eggs, separated
4 tablespoons cornflour (cornstarch)
150 g (5½ oz) caster (superfine) sugar
75 g (2¾ oz) dark muscovado sugar
pinch of salt

**Italian meringue**
165 g (6 oz) caster (superfine) sugar
1 tablespoon glucose syrup
150 ml (5½ fl oz) filtered water
3 large egg whites, at room temperature
pinch of salt
pinch of cream of tartar

1. For the chocolate cake, preheat the oven to 190°C (375°F/Gas 5) and line a 20 × 30 cm (8 × 12 in) greased baking tin with baking paper.

2. Place the butter and chocolate in a heatproof bowl and set over a saucepan of boiling water. Stir with a spatula until almost melted, then remove from the heat and continue to stir until melted completely. Leave to cool slightly.

3. Place the egg yolks in a large mixing bowl and the egg whites in the bowl of an electric mixer. Sift the cornflour into the bowl with the egg yolks, add the caster sugar, muscovado sugar and salt and mix until smooth, then stir in the melted butter and chocolate to form a smooth batter.

4. Turn the electric mixer onto the highest setting and whisk the egg whites until they form soft peaks. Fold the egg whites gradually into the chocolate mixture, then pour the batter into the prepared baking tin. Bake for 40 minutes or until a skewer inserted into the middle of the cake comes out clean, then remove the cake from the oven, place a 340 ml (11½ fl oz/1⅓ cups) dariole mould in the centre and use it as a template to cut out a circle of sponge. Transfer the cut sponge to a wire rack and leave to cool (eat the remainder – it's delicious on its own), then transfer to a suitable container until needed.

5. Fill a 340 ml (11½ fl oz/1⅓ cups) pre-cooled dariole mould with the raspberry and rose gelato, pushing it down firmly with a spoon to ensure there are no air pockets and flattening it with a spatula or palette knife. Transfer to the freezer for 2 hours to harden.

6. Once the gelato has hardened, briefly place the mould gelato-side up (and being sure that no water touches the gelato) in a container of warm water. Remove the mould from the water, turn it upside down and rub it with a wet cloth, scraping the rim of the mould with a paring knife to remove the gelato from the mould (if it doesn't come out repeat this process until it does). Place the moulded gelato on top of the sponge circle, then transfer the bombe to a stainless steel tray and return to the freezer for at least 3 hours, or until needed.

*Continues on following page*

7   45 minutes before you are ready to serve, make the Italian meringue. Whisk the sugar, glucose syrup and water together in a saucepan over a high heat until combined. Insert a sugar thermometer and bring the syrup to 248°C (480°F).

8   Meanwhile, put the egg whites, salt and cream of tartar in the clean bowl of an electric mixer and start whisking the eggs on slow speed. Whisk until the egg whites are frothy and starting to form soft peaks.

9   Increase the speed to high and slowly pour the sugar syrup over in a thin stream, whisking all the while until all the syrup is used. Continue to whisk on high speed for 30 minutes, until the bowl feels cold and the meringue is smooth, glossy and holding stiff peaks. Transfer the meringue to a piping bag with a medium-sized nozzle attached.

10  Remove the hardened bombe from the freezer and immediately pipe the meringue over to cover completely – starting from the bottom of the cake and going up to the top and being careful not to leave any gaps in between pipings. (Don't delay this step as the meringue won't be smooth if you do). Use a blowtorch to give the meringue a nice caramelised colour. Serve immediately.

## Strawberry and watermelon frullato
### *Frullato alle fragole e anguria*

**Serves 1**

**Ingredients:**
400 g (14 oz/4 scoops) Strawberry
    sorbetto (page 66)
juice of 1 lime
200 ml (7 fl oz) freshly squeezed
    watermelon juice

*Frullato is like a dairy-free frappé. You can get it in most gelaterias in Italy, where they blend fresh fruit with sorbet and maybe some fruit juice. This is my version with strawberry sorbet and watermelon juice. It has a thick consistency from the sorbet, almost like a slurpee.*

1   Add all the ingredients to a blender and blend until smooth. Pour into a cup and enjoy with a straw.

## Raspberry and rose gelato
### *Gelato al lampone e rose*

**Makes 1 kg (2 lb 3 oz/10 scoops)**

**Ingredients:**
135 g (5 oz) caster (superfine) sugar
35 g (1¼ oz) dextrose
20 g (¾ oz) skim milk powder
5 g (¼ oz) carob bean powder
645 g (1 lb 7 oz) milk
165 ml (5½ fl oz) pouring (single/light)
    cream
100 g (3½ oz) fresh raspberries
5 g (¼ oz) rosewater

*This is a gelato that I created specifically to use in our summery Bombe alaska (page 72). I think the rose flavour goes really well with berries and the raspberry flavour is quite tart so it matches well with the creamy meringue. I use rosewater here, which adds a really nice perfumed character to the gelato.*

1   Put the sugar, dextrose and skim milk powder in a bowl and mix to combine.

2   Put the carob bean powder in a separate bowl. Add 2 tablespoons of the sugar mixture and mix together well.

3   Pour the milk and cream into a large heavy-based saucepan over a medium heat. Whisk in the carob bean powder mixture and continue to heat, whisking in the sugar mixture as you go, until it hits 85°C (185°F). Remove from the heat, pour into a suitable lidded container and leave to cool in the freezer for 1 hour, or until the mixture drops to 4°C (39°F).

4   Turn on your gelato maker so it begins the freezing process.

5   Add the raspberries and rosewater to the mixture and blend with a hand-held blender until smooth.

6   Pour the mixture into your gelato maker. Once the mixture reaches −4°C (25°F) or is the consistency of soft-serve ice cream (this should take about 30–45 minutes) detach the canister or scoop the gelato into a pre-cooled lidded container. Transfer to the freezer and leave for at least 1 hour to harden before serving.

Caro Carlo sono in viaggio
per la mia meta dove sono
orgolioso di andare. Sono in
una tradotta dove si sta bene
Lì abbiamo tutte le nostre
comodità così farò un bel
viaggetto. Ti scriverò sempre
dove potrò e come potrò.
Per esempio ora scuso se scrivo
male ma il treno non permette
di meglio.
Termino e per ultimo ti dico
Ritornerò dopo di aver
fatto il mio dovere sicuramente

**Prosecco-poached peach with milk gelato and hazelnut croccante**
*Pesca affogata nel prosecco con gelato al fior di latte
e croccanti di nocciole*

**Serves 6**

**Ingredients:**
**600 g (1 lb 5 oz/6 scoops) Milk gelato
(page 30)**

**Hazelnut croccante**
**2 tablespoons glucose syrup**
**135 g (5 oz) caster (superfine) sugar**
**135 g (5 oz) crushed hazelnuts**

**Prosecco-poached peaches**
**150 g (5½ oz) caster (superfine) sugar**
**750 ml (25½ fl oz/3 cups) prosecco**
**1 vanilla bean, split lengthways and
seeds scraped**
**6 peaches, halved and stones removed**

*This dish was inspired by a dish that I ate at Kylie Kwong's restaurant in Sydney where she'd teamed poached fruit (apples, I think) with a brittle (or 'croccante' in Italian). I loved the textures of the dish, the soft fruit and the crunchiness of the brittle. I have used peaches – usually white peaches but just use the best ones you can find – and then added a creamy milk gelato because everything tastes better with gelato, right?*

1   For the hazelnut croccante, add the glucose syrup and caster sugar to a small saucepan over a high heat. Cook, stirring, until caramelised and very dark brown in colour, then add the hazelnuts and mix together thoroughly. Carefully tip the mixture out onto the centre of a heatproof silicone mat, cover with non-stick baking paper and roll out with a rolling pin as thin as possible. Leave to cool, then pull off the paper and chop into small pieces. Set aside until needed.

2   Preheat the oven to 190°C (375°F/Gas 5).

3   For the prosecco-poached peaches, measure the sugar, prosecco and vanilla seeds into an ovenproof dish and mix to combine. Place the peach halves in the baking dish skin-side up and bake for 10 minutes, then turn them over and cook for a further 5 minutes, until the peaches are soft but are still holding their shape. Remove the peaches from the dish and set aside.

4   Strain the cooking liquor and add it to a heavy-based saucepan over a medium heat. Bring to a simmer and reduce by half.

5   To serve, divide the peach halves among bowls, spoon over a little of the reduced liquor and top each with a scoop of milk gelato and a sprinkling of chopped croccante.

# Mascarpone, berry and biscotti gelato
*Gelato al mascarpone, bacche e biscotti*

**Makes 1 kg (2 lb 3 oz/10 scoops)**

**Ingredients:**
120 g (4½ oz) caster (superfine) sugar
50 g (1¾ oz) dextrose
15 g (½ oz) skim milk powder
3 g (1/8 oz) carob bean powder
485 g (1 lb 1 oz) milk
125 ml (4 fl oz/½ cup) pouring (single/
    light) cream
25 g (1 oz) filtered water
25 g (1 oz) egg yolk
150 g (5½ oz) mascarpone

**Chocolate and hazelnut biscotti**
3 eggs
175 g (6 oz) caster (superfine) sugar
250 g (9 oz/1⅓ cups) plain (all-purpose)
    flour
2 tablespoons Dutch (unsweetened)
    cocoa powder
½ teaspoon bicarbonate of soda
    (baking soda)
125 g (4½ oz) roasted hazelnuts

**Raspberry sauce**
200 g (7 oz) fresh raspberries
2 tablespoons filtered water
40 g (1½ oz) caster (superfine) sugar

*Mascarpone adds a rich, almost cheesy creaminess to gelato, while biscotti adds both texture and flavour. The biscotti I use in this recipe is a chocolate and hazelnut version which goes well with berries. Biscotti is easy to make but you need to be careful to cook it for the right amount of time for it to dry out to the right crunchy consistency. To make a plain mascarpone gelato for a Tiramisu layer cake (page 158), make this up as below without adding either the biscotti or berries.*

1    Preheat the oven to 200°C (400°F/Gas 6). Line a baking tray with baking paper.

2    For the chocolate and hazelnut biscotti, add the eggs and sugar to a bowl and whisk together until combined. Sift over the flour, cocoa powder and bicarbonate of soda and stir to form a smooth dough, then add the roasted hazelnuts and mix together with your hands until the nuts are evenly distributed throughout.

3    Turn the dough out onto a clean, floured work surface and divide into two equal-sized pieces. Roll the dough out into log shapes, then transfer to the prepared baking tray and bake for 15 minutes. Remove from the oven and leave to cool on a wire rack for 10–15 minutes, then cut each log into 2 cm (¾ in) pieces using a serrated knife.

4    Arrange the biscotti pieces on the baking tray on one of their cut sides, then return to the oven and bake for a further 10 minutes, turning halfway through cooking, until dried out. Remove from the oven and leave to cool on a wire rack.

5    For the raspberry sauce, add all the ingredients to a heavy-based saucepan over a medium–low heat. Cook for 15 minutes, stirring occasionally to ensure it doesn't catch on the bottom, until the berries have broken down into a sauce and the mixture has reduced and thickened enough to coat the back of a spoon.

6    Pour into a bowl and leave to chill in the fridge until needed.

7    Put the sugar, dextrose and skim milk powder in a bowl and mix to combine. Put the carob bean powder in a separate bowl. Add 2 tablespoons of the sugar mixture and mix together well.

*Continues on following page*

8    Add the milk, cream, water and egg yolk to a large heavy-based saucepan over a medium heat and whisk to combine. Whisk in the carob bean powder mixture and continue to heat, whisking in the sugar mixture as you go, until it hits 85°C (185°F).

9    Remove the pan from the heat, add the mascarpone and blend with a hand-held blender until smooth, then pour into a suitable lidded container and leave to cool in the freezer for 1 hour, or until the mixture drops to 4°C (39°F).

10   Turn on your gelato maker so it begins the freezing process. Transfer the raspberry sauce and biscotti to the freezer to chill.

11   Pour the mixture into your gelato maker. Once the mixture reaches –4°C (25°F) or is the consistency of soft-serve ice cream (this should take about 30–45 minutes) detach the canister or scoop the gelato into a pre-cooled lidded container. Place the gelato in a freezer for 30 minutes to harden further.

12   Roughly chop the chilled biscotti and add to the gelato with the chilled raspberry sauce. Mix together roughly (you want a ripple effect here, so be sure not to overwork the gelato), then transfer to the freezer and leave for at least 1 hour to harden before serving.

Summer
*Estaté*

**Blood plum sorbetto**
*Sorbetto alle prugne rosse*

**Makes 1 kg (2 lb 3 oz/10 scoops)**

**Ingredients:**
**600 g (1 lb 5 oz) blood plums, stoned**
**and cut into small pieces**
**185 g (6½ oz) filtered water**
**5 g (¼ oz) carob bean powder**
**210 g (7½ oz) caster (superfine) sugar**

*This is one of my favourite sorbetto flavours – I can't go past its colour, texture and refreshing taste. I love seeing the skin here because it shows that you have used real ingredients and it's like you're eating the actual fruit; I really don't like it when you taste a sorbetto and you can tell that the fruit used has been cooked or was frozen, as you don't get that same fresh 'realness'.*

1  Put the plum pieces and water in a bowl and blend with a hand-held blender until smooth.

2  Put the carob bean powder in a separate bowl. Add 2 tablespoons of the sugar and mix together well.

3  Gradually add the carob powder and sugar mixture to the plum mixture, blending all the while, until well combined. Add the rest of the sugar and blend to incorporate, then transfer to a suitable lidded container and leave to cool in the freezer for 15–20 minutes, or until the mixture drops to 4°C (39°F).

4  Turn on your gelato maker so it begins the freezing process.

5  Pour the mixture into your gelato maker. Once the mixture reaches –4°C (25°F) (this should take about 30–60 minutes) detach the canister or scoop the gelato into a pre-cooled lidded container. Transfer to the freezer and leave for at least 1 hour to harden before serving.

## Blood plum sorbetto with hot crema
*Sorbetto alle prugne rosse con crema calda*

**Serves 4**

**Ingredients:**
400 g (14 oz/4 scoops) Blood plum
    sorbetto (page 82)

**Hot crema**
250 ml (8½ fl oz/1 cup) pouring (single/
    light) cream
2 egg yolks
2 tablespoons caster (superfine) sugar
2 teaspoons cornflour (cornstarch)
1 vanilla bean, split lengthways and
    seeds scraped

*When I worked at the Gelateria Alberto Marchetti in Turin they had a menu of different affogatos. Affogato is traditionally made with coffee so this was their interpretation of it. You could pick a gelato flavour and mix something with it such as chocolate sauce or crema, similar to a hot custard. The custard reminded me of my grandma. When we were kids, she'd always serve custard with stewed fruit, often plums, and so this dish is a combination of those two memories. I love the colour of this sorbetto, the deep, deep red that comes from the fruit, with nothing else added.*

1    To make the hot crema, add the cream, egg yolks and caster sugar to a heatproof bowl. Sift over the cornflour and whisk everything together until combined, then stir in the vanilla seeds.

2    Transfer the crema mixture to a double boiler set over a medium heat and whisk until thick enough to coat the back of a spoon.

3    To serve, add a scoop of blood plum sorbetto to the centre of a serving bowl and pour the hot crema around the sides. Repeat with the remaining sorbetto and sauce as necessary.

**TIP** The crema here can also be served cold if you like: once thickened, transfer it to the fridge and leave it to chill until needed.

**Mango sorbetto**
*Sorbetto al mango*

**Makes 1 kg (2 lb 3 oz/10 scoops)**

**Ingredients:**
**400 g (14 oz) mango flesh**
**380 g (13½ oz) filtered water**
**2.5 g (⅛ oz) carob bean powder**
**220 g (8 oz) caster (superfine) sugar**

*Who doesn't love mango? It has to be one of the most popular flavours and there's nothing more exciting than when the weather starts to get warm and you see mangoes appearing at the grocery stores. It's a sign that the most fun time of year has arrived.*

1   Put the mango and water in a bowl and blend with a hand-held blender until smooth.

2   Put the carob bean powder in a separate bowl. Add 2 tablespoons of the sugar and mix together well.

3   Gradually add the carob powder and sugar mixture to the mango mixture, blending all the while, until well combined. Add the rest of the sugar and blend to incorporate, then transfer to a suitable lidded container and leave to cool in the freezer for 15–20 minutes, or until the mixture drops to 4°C (39°F).

4   Turn on your gelato maker so it begins the freezing process.

5   Pour the mixture into your gelato maker. Once the mixture reaches –4°C (25°F) (this should take about 30 minutes) detach the canister or scoop the gelato into a pre-cooled lidded container. Transfer to the freezer and leave for at least 1 hour to harden before serving.

**Mango sorbetto with white chocolate mousse**
*Sorbetto al mango con mousse al cioccolato bianco*

**Serves 8**

Ingredients:
**800 g (1 lb 12 oz/8 scoops) Mango
sorbetto (page 86)**

**White chocolate mousse**
**175 g (6 oz) white chocolate, broken into
small chunks**
**4 egg yolks**
**50 g (1¾ oz) caster (superfine) sugar**
**400 ml (13½ fl oz) pouring (single/light)
cream**
**1 teaspoon gelatine powder**
**1–2 tablespoons filtered water**

*This is another recipe that's all about sourcing the best fruit. The smell of a mango is the best test. They have a strong, sweet smell when they're really ripe. Don't use them underripe because they can be sour. White chocolate is a great match with the sweet, tart mango and though this is a really easy dessert to make, it seems to impress people so it's a good one to pull out at a dinner party.*

1    To make the white chocolate mousse, melt the white chocolate in a double boiler or microwave.

2    Add the egg yolks and sugar to the bowl of an electric mixer with the whisk attachment added and beat together until thick, pale and doubled in volume.

3    Whisk the cream in a bowl until soft peaks form.

4    Add the gelatine to a small bowl, cover with the water and stir until the gelatine is dissolved. Add a few spoonfuls of the beaten egg yolk mixture to the gelatine and mix together, then spoon this mixture into the bowl of the electric mixer with the rest of the beaten egg yolks and beat to combine. Pour in the melted white chocolate, beating as you go, then fold in the whipped cream to form a light, airy mousse.

5    Spoon the mousse into eight serving bowls and transfer to the fridge to chill until set. When ready to serve, take the mousse out of the fridge and top each bowl with a scoop of mango gelato.

torna a

Summer
*Estaté*

**Fresh mint gelato**
*Gelato alla menta fresca*

**Makes 1 kg (2 lb 3 oz/10 scoops)**

**Ingredients:**
**115 g (4 oz) caster (superfine) sugar**
**30 g (1 oz) dextrose**
**15 g (½ oz) skim milk powder**
**5 g (¼ oz) carob bean powder**
**550 g (1 lb 3 oz) milk**
**195 ml (6½ fl oz) pouring (single/light)
    cream**
**35 g (1¼ oz) fresh mint leaves**
**90 g (3 oz) condensed milk**

*This has been one of my favourite gelato flavours since I first tasted it when working at Donovans. With this recipe you blend the mint with the base gelato mixture so you get a beautiful pale green colour as well as the refreshing mint flavour. Pay attention when straining the mixture because any pieces of mint leaves that are left can give the gelato a gritty texture. This is great with chocolate – sauce, pudding or cake.*

1   Put the sugar, dextrose and skim milk powder in a bowl and mix to combine.

2   Put the carob bean powder in a separate bowl. Add 2 tablespoons of the sugar mixture and mix together well.

3   Pour the milk and cream into a large heavy-based saucepan over a medium heat. Whisk in the carob bean powder mixture and continue to heat, whisking in the sugar mixture as you go, until it hits 85°C (185°F). Remove from the heat, pour into a suitable lidded container and leave to cool in the freezer for 1 hour, or until the mixture drops to 4°C (39°F).

4   Turn on your gelato maker so it begins the freezing process.

5   Add the mint and condensed milk to the mixture and blend with a hand-held blender until smooth.

6   Strain the mixture and transfer it to your gelato maker. Once it reaches –4°C (25°F) or is the consistency of soft-serve ice cream (this should take about 30–45 minutes) detach the canister or scoop the gelato into a pre-cooled lidded container. Transfer to the freezer and leave for at least 1 hour to harden before serving.

**Passionfruit pavlova with fresh mint gelato and coconut**
*Pavlova al frutto della passione con gelato al cocco e
menta fresca*

*My mum has always made great pavlova. The meringue recipe here is
hers – it's brittle on the outside and nice and chewy inside. It's the cornflour
that brings the chewiness. I think the mint gelato goes really well with the
passionfruit flavours here.*

**Serves 6**

**Ingredients:**

300 ml (10 fl oz) pouring (single/light)
    cream

2 tablespoons desiccated
    (shredded) coconut

600 g (1 lb 5 oz/6 scoops) Fresh mint
    gelato (page 94)

**Meringue**

4 egg whites

pinch of salt

340 g (12 oz) caster (superfine) sugar

4 teaspoons cornflour (cornstarch)

2 teaspoons white vinegar

½ teaspoon vanilla paste

**Passionfruit curd**

3 eggs

2 egg yolks

220 g (8 oz) caster (superfine) sugar

125 ml (4 fl oz/½ cup) passionfruit pulp

150 g (5½ oz) unsalted butter, cubed

**Passionfruit jelly**

4 gelatine leaves or 6 g (¼ oz) gelatine
    powder

150 ml (5 fl oz) filtered water

55 g (2 oz) caster (superfine) sugar

250 ml (8½ fl oz/1 cup) passionfruit pulp,
    strained

1   Preheat the oven to 135°C (275°F/Gas 1). Line a baking tray
    with baking paper.

2   For the meringue, add the egg whites and salt to the clean bowl
    of an electric mixer with the whisk attachment added. On a
    medium speed, whisk the egg whites to soft peaks. Continuing
    to whisk, add the sugar a teaspoon at a time, then add the
    cornflour, white vinegar and vanilla paste and whisk for 15
    minutes to form soft peaks.

3   Spoon six equal-sized dollops of meringue out onto the
    prepared baking tray, leaving 2 cm (¾ in) between them to
    allow them to expand and making an indentation in the middle
    of each with a teaspoon. Bake for 1 hour, then turn the oven off
    and leave the meringues to cool completely in the oven before
    removing. Set aside.

4   To make the passionfruit curd, add the eggs, egg yolks, caster
    sugar and passionfruit pulp to a heatproof bowl and whisk to
    combine. Set the bowl over a saucepan of boiling water and
    gradually add the butter, whisking continuously, until all the
    butter has melted and been incorporated and the mixture has
    thickened enough to coat the back of a spoon. Remove the bowl
    from the heat and pour the curd into a container, then cover
    with plastic wrap and transfer to the fridge to cool.

5   For the passionfruit jelly, place the gelatine leaves in a small
    bowl of ice-cold water and leave them to soften. Place the water
    and sugar in a small heavy-based saucepan over a medium heat
    and stir until the sugar has dissolved, then remove from the
    heat and transfer to a bowl with the passionfruit pulp. Squeeze
    the softened gelatine leaves of excess water, add them to the
    passionfruit mixture and whisk to combine. (If the gelatine
    hasn't dissolved fully, return the mixture to the pan and heat
    gently, whisking until it has.) Pour the mixture into a small tray,
    transfer to the fridge and leave for about 2 hours, or until set.

6   Whip the cream in a bowl using a hand whisk or electric whisk
    until soft peaks form. Place in the fridge until ready to use.

7   To assemble the dessert, divide the meringues among plates.
    Dollop over the whipped cream, spoon over the passionfruit
    curd and top with small teaspoons of the jelly, then sprinkle
    over the desiccated coconut before finishing with a scoop of
    fresh mint gelato.

Summer

*Estaté*

**Makes 1 kg (2 lb 3 oz/10 scoops)**

**Ingredients:**
105 g (3½ oz) caster (superfine) sugar
45 g (1½ oz) dextrose
1 tablespoon skim milk powder
5 g (¼ oz) carob bean powder
515 g (1 lb 2 oz) milk
130 ml (4½ fl oz) pouring (single/light)
    cream
200 g (7 oz) fresh blackberries
80 g (2¾ oz) dark chocolate (70% cocoa
    solids), broken into small chunks
pinch of sea salt flakes

**Blackberry and salted chocolate gelato**
*Gelato alle more e cioccolato salato*

*This was a flavour that I collaborated on with designers Tin & Ed for Valentine's Day. Their brief was mostly about how they wanted it to look good – they wanted it to have a really great colour. The quantity of blackberries in this recipe means that you get exactly that, and the flavour is pretty amazing too.*

1    Put the sugar, dextrose and skim milk powder in a bowl and mix to combine.

2    Put the carob bean powder in a separate bowl. Add 2 tablespoons of the sugar mixture and mix together well.

3    Pour the milk and cream into a large heavy-based saucepan over a medium heat. Whisk in the carob bean powder mixture and continue to heat, whisking in the sugar mixture as you go, until it hits 85°C (185°F). Remove from the heat, pour into a suitable lidded container and leave to cool in the freezer for 1 hour, or until the mixture drops to 4°C (39°F).

4    Turn on your gelato maker so it begins the freezing process.

5    Add the blackberries to the mixture and blend with a hand-held blender until smooth.

6    Strain the mixture to remove the seeds and transfer it to your gelato maker. Once it reaches –4°C (25°F) or is the consistency of soft-serve ice cream (this should take about 30–45 minutes) detach the canister or scoop the gelato into a pre-cooled lidded container. Transfer to the freezer and leave for 1 hour to harden.

7    Melt the chocolate with the salt in a double boiler. Once melted, remove from the heat and leave it to cool to room temperature, then add it to the gelato, drizzling it over and mixing it in with a spatula to break it up into a chip. Place it back in the freezer and leave it for at least 1 hour to harden further before serving.

100—

139

Gelato, and ice cream generally, has always been seen as a seasonal food in Australia, one that you only really think about when the weather turns warm. After spending time in Italy I don't see it that way. I remember when I was a kid we went and visited our nonno and nonna, who were staying in Vicenza, a city in Italy's north-east, near Venice. Nonno was born there and still has family living in the area. It was autumn when we visited them and it was quite cold but they would still take us out to one of the local gelaterias to get gelato. Eating gelato in Italy is just something that you do, no matter what the temperature – it's a social thing.

Obviously when you make gelato with fresh fruit the flavours change with the seasons. As autumn moves in and the weather turns colder, the melons, berries and stone fruits of summer start to disappear so you turn to other fruit, like citrus – oranges, mandarins, lemons, grapefruit and so on, apples and kiwi fruit. The colder months are also when things like nuts and chocolate become more popular. When it's boiling hot in summer, you're probably more likely to want a glass of water than a rich pistachio gelato but when the temperature drops it seems just about right.

Pistachio was the first flavour I worked on when I returned from the gelato course in Bologna. Jamie and I had committed to opening the temporary store and so I had to start developing recipes. The clock was ticking. Some friends of ours had a restaurant in Windsor called Saigon Sally, which had a space upstairs they weren't using so I moved in there with my gelato machinery and started working on the gelati we would be selling at our store. Jamie would come to visit me to see how I was coming along and was always like, 'How come you only have two flavours completed? Are you going to be ready?' I didn't know whether we would be but when we opened in early summer I had more than 50 recipes that I'd worked on over autumn and winter.

I had started with pistachio and then hazelnut gelato because they were mostly about finding the right supplier of the nuts. Getting the best ingredients was the most important thing in making those flavours right and from my time at the gelato university I knew that the best pistachio nuts come from Bronte in Sicily, while the hazelnuts I wanted to use come from Piedmont. I prefer to use pastes for these gelati because the machinery they use to grind the nuts really gets the oils out so the texture of the gelato is quite dense and really creamy. When you try to do it yourself from fresh nuts, you just don't get the same intensity of flavour.

Another ingredient that I love working with in autumn is honey, especially now that we can source it from our own beehives. It's a good time to use the honey because the bees have been producing it all summer but we have to make sure to leave enough for them to survive on over winter. Again, it's a seasonal thing. During the

seven months we had the temporary store in Faraday Street I noticed that there was a guy in a beekeeping suit who kept coming in and out of the house next door. I asked around and eventually met Nic Dowse, who runs Honey Fingers. He'd installed and was looking after the next-door hives so we started talking and ended up trading honey for gelato. Eventually we had Nic install our own hives on our roof and used the honey whenever it was available and started using honeycomb as a topping for gelato. Nic's always up on the roof tending to the bees and he's often in the shop, dressed in his full beekeeping suit, getting some gelato. Last autumn we did a range of gelato under the name Pollination, which was all about the relationship of the bee with the flower. The flavours were rose and honey nougat; lavender, lemon and ricotta; and elderflower and lychee. We've also done similar ranges showcasing local cheesemakers and local chocolate makers.

Some of the other flavours I use when the weather turns colder come from my mother's side of the family, the Lebanese side. My grandfather was from Lebanon and he died when we were young. My grandma wasn't Lebanese (she's from Adelaide) but she took on his culture, and their friends used to say that my grandmother was the best at making Lebanese food. She used to have brunch for all the family on Sundays when we were growing up and she would produce these feasts. Some of those flavours – the spices, rosewater, nuts and honey – I use in my gelato. I like it because of the unique flavours but also because it combines the Lebanese and Italian sides of my heritage.

We opened our second permanent Windsor store in autumn. It had taken longer to get finished than the first one so we missed out on the summer opening we had at Pidapipó in Carlton. The weather was still warm but the nights were getting colder and we didn't know if people would still be wanting to come and eat gelato in a store that they might not have heard of. I needn't have worried. There have been plenty of nights with people standing outside in their scarves and gloves eating gelato.

**Apple and amaretti crumble with cinnamon and raisin gelato**
*Mele e sbriciolata di amaretti con gelato alla cannella e uvetta*

**Serves 6–8**

**Ingredients:**
110 g (4 oz) amaretti biscuits
95 g (3¼ oz) cold unsalted butter, diced
160 g (5½ oz) plain (all-purpose) flour
45 g (1½ oz) rolled (porridge) oats
190 g (6½ oz) caster (superfine) sugar
5 granny smith apples, peeled, cored
        and cut into small chunks
juice of 1 lemon
½ teaspoon ground cinnamon
1 teaspoon vanilla paste

Cinnamon and raisin gelato
50 g (1¾ oz) raisins
200 g (7 oz) amaretto, or enough to cover
135 g (5 oz) caster (superfine) sugar
35 g (1¼ oz) dextrose
20 g (¾ oz) skim milk powder
5 g (¼ oz) carob bean powder
645 g (1 lb 7 oz) milk
165 ml (5½ fl oz) pouring (single/light)
        cream
5 g (¼ oz) ground cinnamon

*Apple crumble is a natural fit with gelato – it's a classic dessert that everybody seems to love. I've added amaretti to the traditional recipe to give it more of an Italian flavour.*

1 For the cinnamon and raisin gelato, put the raisins in a small container and pour the amaretto over to cover completely. Leave to soak for at least 4 hours.

2 Put the sugar, dextrose and skim milk powder in a bowl and mix to combine.

3 Put the carob bean powder in a separate bowl. Add 2 tablespoons of the sugar mixture and mix together well.

4 Add the milk, cream and cinnamon to a large heavy-based saucepan over a medium heat. Whisk in the carob bean powder mixture and continue to heat, whisking in the sugar mixture as you go, until it hits 85°C (185°F). Remove from the heat, pour into a suitable lidded container and leave to cool in the freezer for 1 hour, or until the mixture drops to 4°C (39°F).

5 Turn on your gelato maker so it begins the freezing process.

6 Pour the mixture into your gelato maker. Once the mixture reaches –4°C (25°F) or is the consistency of soft-serve ice cream (this should take about 30–45 minutes) detach the canister or scoop the gelato into a pre-cooled lidded container. Transfer to the freezer and leave for 1 hour to harden.

7 Drain and chop the raisins, setting aside the raisin-infused amaretto for drinking later, then add them to the gelato and mix together well. Return the gelato to the freezer until needed.

8 Preheat the oven to 180°C (350°F/Gas 4).

9 Place the amaretti biscuits in a large bowl and crush them with the end of a rolling pin to a fine crumb (alternatively, blitz them briefly to a similar consistency in a food processor). Add the diced butter, flour, rolled oats and 110 g (4 oz) of the sugar and mix everything together with the tips of your fingers to form a fine breadcrumb-like texture (be careful not to overwork it as you don't want the mixture to become a dough).

10 Place the apple chunks in a 35 × 25 cm (14 × 10 in) ovenproof dish with the lemon juice, cinnamon, vanilla paste and remaining sugar and mix together well. Spoon over the crumble mixture evenly and bake in the oven for 40-45 minutes, or until the crust is golden brown and the edges of the dish are caramelised. Divide among bowls and serve with scoops of the cinnamon and raisin gelato.

**Pear sorbetto**

*Sorbetto alla pera*

Makes 1 kg (2 lb 3 oz/10 scoops)

Ingredients:

600 g (1 lb 5 oz) pear, cored and diced

150 g (5½ oz) filtered water

5 g (¼ oz) carob bean powder

250 g (9 oz) caster (superfine) sugar

*You can use almost any variety of pear for this recipe but you might want to avoid the brown-skinned varieties because they'll make the colour of the sorbetto a bit dark. I always like to keep the skin on the fruit because it adds to the realness of the flavour. Use green-skinned pears and you'll get a pure white sorbetto with some tiny speckles of green. Very pretty.*

1    Put the pear and water in a bowl and blend with a hand-held blender until smooth.

2    Put the carob bean powder in a separate bowl. Add 2 tablespoons of the sugar and mix together well.

3    Gradually add the carob powder and sugar mixture to the pear mixture, blending all the while, until well combined. Add the rest of the sugar and blend to incorporate, then transfer to a suitable lidded container and leave to cool in the freezer for 1 hour, or until the mixture drops to 4°C (39°F).

4    Turn on your gelato maker so it begins the freezing process.

5    Pour the mixture into your gelato maker. Once the mixture reaches –4°C (25°F) (this should take about 30–40 minutes) detach the canister or scoop the gelato into a pre-cooled lidded container. Transfer to the freezer and leave for at least 1 hour to harden before serving.

**Bomboloni with Nutella swirl gelato**
*Bomboloni con gelato variegato alla Nutella*

Makes 10

Ingredients:

1 kg (2 lb 3 oz/10 scoops) Nutella swirl
        gelato (page 125)
Nutella, to serve

Bomboloni
250 ml (8½ fl oz/1 cup) milk, at room
        temperature
12 g (½ oz) fresh yeast
1 egg
2 large egg yolks
115 g (4 oz/½ cup) caster (superfine)
        sugar, plus 300 g (10½ oz)
        for coating
500 g (1 lb 2 oz/3⅓ cups) plain (all-
        purpose) flour
2 teaspoons salt
zest of 1 lemon
1 teaspoon honey
100 g (3½ oz) cold unsalted butter, cubed
vegetable oil, for frying

*This is something that my brother Jamie has always wanted me to do and
is always pushing me to have as an addition to the menu at Pidapipó. In
Italy you traditionally make this sort of gelato sandwich with brioche but
Jamie likes doughnuts and after trying this one out, I reckon it's a pretty
good idea.*

1   To make the bomboloni, add a third of the milk to a bowl with
    the yeast and stir to dissolve.

2   In a separate bowl, whisk the egg and egg yolks together with
    the rest of the milk to combine. Set aside.

3   Add the sugar, flour, salt, lemon zest and honey to the bowl
    of an electric mixer with the dough hook attached. Over a low
    speed, slowly pour in the egg and milk mixture, and mix for
    2–3 minutes until fully combined, then add the yeast mixture
    and continue to mix for 5 minutes, adding a cube or two of
    the cold butter every few minutes, to form a soft (not sticky)
    dough that is starting to come away from the sides of the bowl.
    Transfer the bowl to a warm spot, cover with plastic wrap and
    leave to rise for 3 hours, or until doubled in size.

4   Once risen, transfer the dough to a clean, floured work surface
    and knock it back, then divide it into ten 60 g (2 oz) pieces and
    roll into rounds. Arrange the pieces on a baking tray lined with
    non-stick baking paper, cover with plastic wrap and leave to
    rise again for 90 minutes, or until doubled in size.

5   Fill a large saucepan half full with vegetable oil and heat to
    170°C (340°F). Carefully lower the bomboloni into the hot oil in
    batches of three at a time and cook for 1–2 minutes on each side
    until golden brown all over.

6   Remove the bomboloni with a slotted spoon and drain on paper
    towel, then roll in sugar until coated on all sides. Eat hot or cold,
    but either way slice the bomboloni in half, placing a scoop of
    Nutella swirl gelato on one side and spreading a little Nutella
    over the other. Sandwich together and serve.

## Crema and jam gelato
### *Gelato alla crema e marmellata*

**Makes 1 kg (2 lb 3 oz/10 scoops)**

**Ingredients:**
185 g (6½ oz) caster (superfine) sugar
20 g (¾ oz) dextrose
10 g (¼ oz) skim milk powder
2 g (⅛ oz) carob bean powder
385 g (13½ oz) milk
100 ml (3½ fl oz) pouring (single/light) cream
150 g (5½ oz) filtered water
140 g (5 oz) egg yolk
1 vanilla bean, split lengthways and seeds scraped

**Strawberry jam sauce**
500 g (1 lb 2 oz) fresh or frozen strawberries, hulled
200 g (7 oz) caster (superfine) sugar

*In this classic gelato flavour the strawberry 'jam' sauce cuts through the richness of the egg yolks nicely. I don't mind using frozen berries to make fruity sauces as you cook them anyway so you lose that fresh berry flavour, while the extra water content they contain helps the fruit to poach properly. You can substitute the strawberries here with any berries – raspberries also work well.*

1   For the strawberry jam sauce, add the strawberries and sugar to a small heavy-based saucepan over a low heat. Cook for 15–20 minutes, stirring occasionally to ensure it doesn't catch on the bottom, until the berries have broken down into a sauce and the mixture has reduced and thickened enough to coat the back of a spoon. Pour into a bowl and leave to chill in the fridge until needed.

2   Put the sugar, dextrose and skim milk powder in a bowl and mix to combine.

3   Put the carob bean powder in a separate bowl. Add 2 tablespoons of the sugar mixture and mix together well.

4   Add the milk, cream, water, egg yolk and vanilla seeds to a large heavy-based saucepan over a medium heat. Whisk in the carob bean powder mixture and continue to heat, whisking in the sugar mixture as you go, until it hits 85°C (185°F). Remove from the heat, pour into a suitable lidded container and leave to cool in the freezer for 1 hour, or until the mixture drops to 4°C (39°F).

5   Turn on your gelato maker so it begins the freezing process.

6   Pour the mixture into your gelato maker. Once the mixture reaches –4°C (25°F) or is the consistency of soft-serve ice cream (this should take about 30–45 minutes) detach the canister or scoop the gelato into a pre-cooled lidded container. Transfer to the freezer and leave for 1 hour to harden.

7   Spoon the chilled jam over the gelato and mix together roughly (you want a ripple effect here, so be sure not to overwork the gelato) then return the gelato to the freezer and leave for at least 1 hour to harden further before serving.

Hunted+
Gathered
Dominican
Republic
Dark Organic
Chocolate
70% Cacao
net 3kg
Hunted+
Gathered
Dominican
Republic
Dark Organic
Chocolate
70% Cacao
net 3kg

**Baker D. Chirico hot cross bun and crema and jam gelato sandwich**
*Hot cross buns del pasticcere D. Chirico e sandwich di gelato alla crema e marmellata*

*This was a collaboration I did with Daniel Chirico from Baker D. Chirico. I made a gelato to go with his hot cross buns – which I think are the best in Melbourne – trying to capture the idea of the butter and jam you usually have with them. I don't use eggs in any of our gelato unless I specifically want to taste the egg; I use them here because I want it to be rich and creamy, like vanilla ice cream. The recipe makes a lovely chocolate hot cross bun but if you want to make these in a hurry, then regular shop-bought buns also work well.*

**Serves 8**

**Ingredients:**
800 g (1 lb 12 oz/8 scoops) Crema and jam gelato (page 119)

**Buns**
500 g (1 lb 2 oz) strong flour
150 g (5½ oz) sugar
10 g (¼ oz) salt
20 g (¾ oz) Dutch (unsweetened) cocoa powder
15 g (½ oz) fresh yeast
100 g (3½ oz) levain (sourdough starter)
325 ml (11 fl oz) milk
75 g (2¾ oz) butter, diced
75 g (2¾ oz) roasted hazelnuts, chopped
250 g (9 oz) dark chocolate (70% cocoa solids), broken into small chunks

**Cross**
50 g (1¾ oz) self-raising flour
50 ml (1¾ fl oz) filtered water
15 g (½ oz) Dutch (unsweetened) cocoa powder

1   For the buns, add the flour, sugar, salt, cocoa powder, yeast, levain and milk to the bowl of a stand mixer with the dough hook attachment added and mix together on low speed for 10 minutes to combine. Add the butter and mix together for a further 8 minutes, then turn the speed up to medium and mix for another 2 minutes to form a dough. Add the chopped hazelnuts and chocolate pieces and mix together for 1 minute to incorporate.

2   Cover the bowl with plastic wrap and leave the dough to rest for 2–3 hours at room temperature.

3   Preheat the oven to 185°C (365°F/Gas 4). Line two baking trays with baking paper.

4   Once rested, divide the dough out into 80 g (2¾ oz) portions, then roll into balls and transfer to the prepared baking trays.

5   For the cross, combine all the ingredients together in a bowl and mix together until smooth. Spoon the mixture into a piping bag with a small nozzle fitted. Pipe a line along each bun, then repeat in the other direction to create crosses.

6   Bake for 20–25 minutes, until golden brown. Remove from the oven and leave to cool slightly, then split each bun in half and add a scoop of crema and jam gelato to the centre of each. Sandwich together and serve immediately.

**Bacio bombe alaska**
*Bombe alaska al bacio*

**Serves 4**

**Ingredients:**
305 g (11 oz) Bacio gelato (page 126)

**Chocolate cake**
175 g (6 oz) unsalted butter, cubed
225 g (8 oz) dark chocolate (70% cocoa
     solids), broken into small chunks
6 eggs, separated
4 tablespoons cornflour (cornstarch)
150 g (5½ oz) caster (superfine) sugar
75 g (2¾ oz) dark muscovado sugar
pinch of salt

**Italian meringue**
165 g (6 oz) caster (superfine) sugar
1 tablespoon glucose syrup
150 ml (5 fl oz) filtered water
3 large egg whites, at room temperature
pinch of salt
pinch of cream of tartar

*This recipe is inspired by my favourite dessert at Donovans, one of the first restaurants I ever worked at. It looks harder than it is, though it does take time to do all the steps. It's a good idea to cook the cake part of the recipe the day before – it makes it easier to put everything together quickly on the day you want to serve it. The Italian meringue might take some practice but nothing beats its creamy, moussey consistency, particularly when you also add chocolate and hazelnut into the mix. I like to serve this at dinner parties. I put it in the middle of the table, give everybody a spoon and tell them to dig in. It may not be elegant but it's a great way to share.*

1    For the chocolate cake, preheat the oven to 190°C (375°F/Gas 5) and line a 20 × 30 cm (8 × 12 in) greased baking tin with baking paper.

2    Place the butter and chocolate in a heatproof bowl and set over a saucepan of boiling water. Stir with a spatula until almost melted, then remove from the heat and continue to stir until melted completely. Leave to cool slightly.

3    Place the egg yolks in a large mixing bowl and the egg whites in the bowl of an electric mixer. Sift the cornflour into the bowl with the egg yolks, add the caster sugar, muscovado sugar and salt and mix until smooth, then stir in the melted butter and chocolate to form a smooth batter.

4    Turn the electric mixer onto the highest setting and whisk the egg whites until they form soft peaks. Fold the egg whites gradually into the chocolate mixture, then pour the batter into the prepared baking tin. Bake for 40 minutes or until a skewer inserted into the middle of the cake comes out clean, then remove the cake from the oven, centre a 340 ml (11½ fl oz/1⅓ cups) dariole mould on the top of the sponge and use it as a template to cut out a circle. Transfer the cut sponge to a wire rack and leave to cool (eat the remainder – it's delicious on its own), then transfer to a suitable container until needed.

5    Fill a 340 ml (11½ fl oz/1⅓ cups) pre-cooled metal dariole mould with the bacio gelato, pushing it down firmly with a spoon to ensure there are no air pockets and flattening it with a spatula or palette knife. Transfer to the freezer for 2 hours to harden.

*Continues on following page*

6    Once the gelato has hardened, place the mould gelato-side up (and being sure that no water touches the gelato), briefly in a container of warm water. Remove the mould from the water, turn it upside down and rub it with a wet cloth, scraping the rim of the mould with a paring knife to remove the gelato from the mould (if it doesn't come out repeat this process until it does). Place the moulded gelato on top of the sponge circle, then transfer the bombe to a stainless steel tray and return to the freezer for at least 3 hours, or until needed.

7    Forty-five minutes before you are ready to serve, make the Italian meringue. Whisk the sugar, glucose syrup and water together in a saucepan over a high heat until combined. Insert a sugar thermometer and bring the syrup to 248°C (480°F).

8    Meanwhile, put the egg whites, salt and cream of tartar in the clean bowl of an electric mixer and start whisking the eggs on slow speed. Whisk until the egg whites are frothy and starting to form soft peaks.

9    Increase the speed to high and slowly pour the sugar syrup over in a thin stream, whisking all the while until the syrup is used. Continue to whisk on high speed for 30 minutes, until the bowl feels cold and the meringue is smooth, glossy and holding stiff peaks. Transfer the meringue to a piping bag with a medium-sized nozzle attached.

10   Remove the hardened bombe from the freezer and immediately pipe over the meringue to cover completely – starting from the bottom of the cake and going up to the top and being careful not to leave any gaps in between pipings. (Don't delay this step as the meringue won't be smooth if you do). Use a blowtorch to give the meringue a nice caramelised colour. Serve immediately.

## Nutella swirl gelato
### *Gelato variegato alla Nutella*

**Makes 1 kg (2 lb 3 oz/10 scoops)**

**Ingredients:**
135 g (5 oz) caster (superfine) sugar
35 g (1¼ oz) dextrose
20 g (¾ oz) skim milk powder
5 g (¼ oz) carob bean powder
645 g (1 lb 7 oz) milk
165 ml (5½ fl oz) pouring (single/light)
    cream
80 g (2¾ oz) Nutella

*This is one of our most popular flavours. You normally associate Nutella with toast, crêpes or pastry but I think it's best in gelato. You need to heat the Nutella up slightly so it's a runny consistency that mixes easily into the gelato.*

1  Put the sugar, dextrose and skim milk powder in a bowl and mix to combine.

2  Put the carob bean powder in a separate bowl. Add 2 tablespoons of the sugar mixture and mix together well.

3  Add the milk and cream to a large heavy-based saucepan over a medium heat. Whisk in the carob bean powder mixture and continue to heat, whisking in the sugar mixture as you go, until it hits 85°C (185°F). Remove from the heat, pour into a suitable lidded container and leave to cool in the freezer for 1 hour, or until the mixture drops to 4°C (39°F).

4  Turn on your gelato maker so it begins the freezing process.

5  Pour the mixture into your gelato maker. Once the mixture reaches −4°C (25°F) or is the consistency of soft-serve ice cream (this should take about 30–45 minutes) detach the canister or scoop the gelato into a pre-cooled lidded container. Transfer to the freezer and leave for 1 hour to harden.

6  Heat the Nutella in a double boiler or microwave until runny. Add the Nutella to the gelato and mix together roughly (you want a ripple effect here, so be sure not to overwork the gelato) then return the gelato to the freezer and leave for at least 1 hour to harden before serving.

## Nutella swirl frappé
### *Frappé variegato alla nutella*

**Serves 1**

**Ingredients:**
300 g (10½ oz/3 scoops) Nutella swirl
    gelato (see above)
200 ml (7 fl oz) milk

*You can use any flavour of gelato you like with this recipe but the Nutella swirl is my favourite. It's really simple – you just blend the gelato with milk. I find old fashioned milkshake machines, like you see in milkbars, are best for blending a frappé because they keep the texture thicker and creamier, but a regular blender will still do the job nicely.*

1  Add the gelato and milk to a blender and blend until smooth. Pour into a cup and enjoy with a straw.

**Bacio gelato**
*Gelato al bacio*

**Makes 1 kg (2 lb 3 oz/10 scoops)**

**Ingredients:**
104 g (3½ oz) caster (superfine) sugar
15 g (½ oz) skim milk powder
15 g (½ oz) dark muscovado sugar
50 g (1¾ oz) dextrose
20 g (¾ oz) Dutch (unsweetened)
    cocoa powder
4 g (¼ oz) carob bean powder
500 g (1 lb 2 oz) milk
130 ml (4½ fl oz) pouring (single/light)
    cream
60 g (2 oz) filtered water
20 g (¾ oz) dark chocolate (70% cocoa
    solids), broken into small chunks
80 g (2¾ oz) hazelnut paste

*Bacio gelato is my personal favourite and is the flavour I would always pick when I was going around to all the gelaterias in Italy.*

1    Put the sugar, skim milk powder, dark muscovado sugar, dextrose and cocoa powder in a bowl and mix to combine.

2    Put the carob bean powder in a separate bowl. Add 2 tablespoons of the sugar mixture and mix together well.

3    Pour the milk, cream and water into a large heavy-based saucepan over a medium heat. Whisk in the carob bean powder mixture and continue to heat, whisking in the sugar mixture as you go, until it hits 85°C (185°F). Remove from the heat, add the chocolate and whisk together until the chocolate has melted into the mixture and everything is well combined.

4    Add the hazelnut paste and blend with a hand-held blender until smooth, then pour into a suitable lidded container and leave to cool in the freezer for 1 hour, or until the mixture drops to 4°C (39°F).

5    Turn on your gelato maker so it begins the freezing process.

6    Pour the mixture into your gelato maker. Once the mixture reaches –4°C (25°F) or is the consistency of soft-serve ice cream (this should take about 30–45 minutes) detach the canister or scoop the gelato into a pre-cooled lidded container. Transfer to the freezer and leave for at least 1 hour to harden before serving.

Autumn
*Autumno*

**Peanut butter and chocolate fudge gelato**
*Gelato al burro d'arachidi e fondente al cioccolato*

**Makes 1 kg (2 lb 3 oz/10 scoops)**

**Ingredients:**
135 g (5 oz) caster (superfine) sugar
35 g (1¼ oz) dextrose
20 g (¾ oz) skim milk powder
5 g (¼ oz) carob bean powder
645 g (1 lb 7 oz) milk
165 ml (5½ fl oz) pouring (single/light) cream
125 g (4½ oz) smooth good-quality peanut butter
½ quantity Chocolate fudge sauce (page 49), at room temperature

*While this is a perfect gelato for eating on its own, it also pairs up with the cookies on page 128 to create an even more indulgent dessert. Peanut butter and chocolate are a perfect match and I've found that people really love these heavy, rich flavours during the colder months.*

1   Put the sugar, dextrose and skim milk powder in a bowl and mix to combine.

2   Put the carob bean powder in a separate bowl. Add 2 tablespoons of the sugar mixture and mix together well.

3   Add the milk and cream to a large heavy-based saucepan over a medium heat. Whisk in the carob bean powder mixture and continue to heat, whisking in the sugar mixture as you go, until it hits 85°C (185°F). Add the peanut butter and blend with a hand-held blender until smooth, then pour into a suitable lidded container and leave to cool in the freezer for 1 hour, or until the mixture drops to 4°C (39°F).

4   Turn on your gelato maker so it begins the freezing process.

5   Pour the mixture into your gelato maker. Once the mixture reaches –4°C (25°F) or is the consistency of soft-serve ice cream (this should take about 30–45 minutes) detach the canister or scoop the gelato into a pre-cooled lidded container. Transfer to the freezer and leave for 1 hour to harden.

6   Add the fudge sauce to the gelato and mix it together roughly (you want a ripple effect here, so be sure not to overwork the gelato) then return the gelato to the freezer and leave for at least 1 hour to harden further before serving.

**Peanut butter and chocolate fudge cookie sandwich**
*Gelato sandwich al burro d'arachidi e fondente al cioccolato*

**Serves 5**

**Ingredients:**

500 g (1 lb 2 oz/5 scoops) Peanut
    butter and chocolate fudge gelato
    (page 127)

**Peanut butter and chocolate cookies**

170 g (6 oz) unsalted butter

200 g (7 oz) caster (superfine) sugar

3 tablespoons glucose syrup

175 g (6 oz) smooth good-quality
    peanut butter

1 egg

1 egg yolk

1 teaspoon vanilla extract

100 g (3½ oz/⅔ cup) plain (all-purpose)
    flour

50 g (1¾ oz) milk chocolate chips

½ teaspoon baking powder, sifted

*These were designed for an event we did that required me to come up with something exclusively for the occasion. The cookie sandwich is something they do in Italy. It's an easy, fun way to eat gelato. The peanut butter and chocolate fudge gelato is sandwiched between two peanut butter cookies that need to have a soft texture to make eating it easier. The event I made these for was a bit of a nightmare, but I was really pleased with the sandwich.*

1    Line a baking tray with non-stick baking paper.

2    To make the peanut butter and chocolate cookies, place the butter, sugar and glucose syrup in the bowl of an electric mixer with the paddle attachment added and beat for 5 minutes, or until pale and creamy. Add the peanut butter, egg, egg yolk and vanilla extract and beat until combined, then add the flour, chocolate chips and baking powder and beat to form a dough.

3    Using a 90 ml (3 fl oz) ice cream scoop, scoop out a ball of the dough and place it on the prepared baking tray, then flatten it slightly with your hands. Repeat, leaving a gap of at least 2 cm (¾ in) between cookies, until you have 10 cookies on the tray. Cover with plastic wrap and leave to chill and firm in the fridge for at least 2 hours.

4    Preheat the oven to 180°C (350°F/Gas 4).

5    Once chilled, transfer the tray to the hot oven and bake the cookies for 15–18 minutes or until the outside looks crisp. Remove from the oven and leave to cool on a wire rack.

6    To serve, place a scoop of the peanut butter and chocolate fudge gelato on the bottom side of one of the cookies, then lay another cookie, bottom-side down, on top and sandwich together. Eat straight away.

**TIP** You can make up these cookie sandwiches a few hours in advance and store them on a tray in the freezer; just don't leave them there too long or the cookies will become soggy.

Nel Centenario della nasc

dal Comitato Italiano di Coordinamen

del Capo dell'opposizione Statal

# SETTIMANA

## CALENDARIO D

## LUNEDI' 27 MAGGIO

### ORE 3 P.M. - VISITA AL ROYAL MELBOURNE HOSPITAL

Come ogni anno, rappresentanti della Comunità italiana si recheranno negli ospedali di Melbourne per far sentire anche in quei luoghi di sofferenza e di dolore, agli ammalati italiani e al personale che per essi si adopera con grande spirito di abnegazione, la fraterna solidarietà della comunità tutta. In quest'opera altamente umana e toccante si prodigherà la signorina Daniela De Felicibus, «Miss Italian Community 1973» accompagnata, di volta in volta, dai presidenti e dalle delegazioni dei vari club italiani di Melbourne.

La prima visita avrà luogo al Royal Melbourne Hospital, lunedì 27 maggio, alle ore 3 p.m. In tale occasione «Miss Italian Community 1973» sarà accompagnata dal presidente del C.I.C., avv. Luciano Bini e dalla delegazione del Bari S.C. che consegnerà una bandiera italiana all'ospedale.

### ORE 4.30 P.M. - VISITA AL ST. FRANCIS XAVIER CABRINI HOSPITAL

La delegazione dell'Ibleo S.C. accompagnerà la Miss Italian Community 1973 nella visita al St. Francis Xavier Cabrini.

### ORE 6 P.M. - MOSTRA D'ARTE - DILETTANTI F.C.I.

Dalle 6,00 alle 9,00 p.m. presso la sala di St. Brigida sarà aperta al pubblico la Mostra d'Arte-Dilettanti della F.C.I.

### ORE 7.30 P.M. PRESENTAZIONE DI LIBRI ITALIANI

Presso la sede dei Circolo Cavour, 172 Cecil St., South Melbourne, presentazione di libri italiani al Sindaco di South Melbourne, alla scuola secondaria Brunswick Girl's High School ed alla Preside signora D.J. English. La presentazione avrà inizio alle 7,30 p.m.

Holding, il Console Generale d'Italia, Dr. I. Argento, e il sindaco di Melbourne, Cr. Whalley.

Il Ballo Nazionale richiamerà certamente anche la parte più attiva della comunità italiana, i presidenti di moltissimi club e gli esponenti italiani più in vista dei settori commerciali e industriali di Melbourne, dove essi sempre si sono fatti onore con il loro spirito di intraprendenza, l'onestà e la serietà del loro lavoro.

La manifestazione sarà allietata dalle orchestre «La Strada» di Sam Bottari e «The Burlington Lodge». I biglietti al prezzo di dollari 10 ciascuno (vino incluso) si possono ancora richiedere a:

Tutte le Segreterie di Clubs e Associazioni di Melbourne, C.I.C. 612 Nicholson Street North Fitzroy, Tel. 489 2089.

## MERCOLEDI' 29 MAGGIO

### ORE 10 A.M. - DIMOSTRAZIONE ARTE CULINARIA E «WINE TASTING»

Nell'Auditorium del Gas and Fuel Corporation (Princess Gate, 171 Flinders St.) dalle ore 10,00 a.m. alle ore 12,00 avrà luogo una dimostrazione di arte culinaria ed un «Wine Tasting» cortesemente offerto dalle Distillerie Stock di Melbourne.

### ORE 2,30 P.M. - VISITA AL ST. VINCENT HOSPITAL

La delegazione del Lazio S.C. e del Floridia Club, accompagneranno la Miss Italian Community nella visita al St. Vincent's Hospital.

### ORE 3,30 P.M. - VISITA AL SACRED HEART HOSPITAL

La Miss Italian Community 1973, accompagnata dalla delegazione del Vizzini Social Club visiterà il Sacred Heart Hospital.

### ORE 4.30 P.M. - VISITA AL ROYAL CHILDREN'S HOSPITAL

pagliacci
spetta

## GIO

Visita
Welfare C
ral Hospi

### C

Nel «M
terrà il s
alle 7,30

### ORE 7.3

Presso
St., Fitz
dentesca

### ORE 8,1

Il Teat
al Princ
Melbourn
N. Manza
colo inizi

## VEN

### ORE 1 P

Alla 1,
Club, 10
per gli u
interverr
Estero O

### ORE 8.15

Nel G
Melbourn
«premiere
spettacolo

### ORE 8.1

...lielmo Marconi, organizzata

...il patrocinio del Premier del Victoria,

...sole Generale d'Italia e dell'O.T.C.

# ...TALIANA '74

## MANIFESTAZIONI

...usticana». Lo
...8,00 p.m.

...AGGIO

...N
...AL
...dell'Italian
...Western Gene-

...ING»
...ion Centre si
...» dalle 6,00

...UDENTESCA
...gh (Falconer
...a serata stu-
...m.

...COLO TEA-
...ne presenterà
...University of
...commedia di
...». Lo spetta-

...AGGIO

...ER UOMINI

...Veneto Social
...en, colazione
...i, alla quale
...Commercio

...FILM «MIMI
...n Building -
...presentato in
...llurgico». Lo
...5 ...m.

...COLO

Cultura (Il Melbourne Arts Centre si trova in St. Kilda Rd. Melbourne).

### ORE 8 P.M. - SPETTACOLO TEATRALE

Il Gruppo Teatrale Italiano presenterà «La finta ammalata di Carlo Goldoni nella Tecnical School Hall, Derby St., Sunshine. Lo spettacolo iniziera alle ore 8,00 p.m.

### ORE 8.15 P.M. - SPETTACOLO TEATRALE

Alle ore 8,15 p.m. nel Prince Philip Theatre, ultima rappresentazione della commedia di N. Manzari «Partita a quattro», presentata dal Teatro Stabile di Melbourne.

## DOMENICA 2 GIUGNO

### ORE 11 A.M. MESSA ITALIANA

La tradizionale Messa Italiana, alle ore 11 a.m. nella Cattedrale di S. Patrizio richiamera anche quest'anno, come sempre, migliaia di connazionali, gli studenti delle scuole cattoliche delle varie parrocchie, tutte le associazioni italiane di Melbourne con bandiere e stendardi ed un folto stuolo di ragazze in costumi folkloristici delle varie regioni d'Italia. La Messa Solenne sara officiata da Sua Eccellenza Monsignor Gino Parro, Pro-Nunzio Apostolico, e concelebrata assieme a prelati italiani e australiani.

### ORE 3 P.M. - INCONTRO DI CALCIO

Alle 3,00 p.m. nell'Olympic Park, Swan St., Melbourne, avra luogo l'incontro di calcio Juventus Alexander.

### ORE 8 P.M. - SMORGASBORD DINNER DANCE

Nella sede del Veneto Social Club (101 Bulleen Rd., Bulleen) avra luogo un Dinner Dance con somorgasbord, con inizio alle 8,00 p.m.

## Altre manifestazioni

Mostra e presentazione di libri italiani allo Swinburne College of Technology.

«Pic-nic delle castagne» organizzato dagli studenti universitari.

### SETTIMANA ITALIANA ALLO SWIMBURNE COLLEGE OF TECHNOLOGY

Gli oltre 250 studenti dello Swimburne College of Technology hanno voluto celebrare quest'anno la Festa della Repubblica Italiana con una «Settimana Italiana» loro propria che comprende le seguenti manifestazioni:

**Lunedì 3 giugno,** dalle ore 6 alle ore 8,30 p.m. picnic delle castagne (vino incluso) - Prezzo di partecipazione, cents 80 a persona;

**Martedì 4 giugno,** discorsi di J. Sgro e della signora Salerno;

**Mercoledì 5 giugno,** Pizza and Wine Night, dalle ore 8 p.m. alle ore 12 p.m. nel ristorante «Il Gambero» (215 Lygon St, Carlton). Prezzo di partecipazione dollari 2 a persona;

**Giovedì 6 giugno,** proiezione cinematografica del film «La moglie del prete», dalle ore 8 p.m. alle ore 12 p.m., nell'Ethel Hall a cui seguira una «Supper Night». Prezzo di partecipazione: studenti dollari 1; non studenti dollari 1,50;

**Venerdì 7 giugno,** Dinner-dance nella Piccola San Remo, in Capel St., North Melbourne, con inizio alle ore 7,30 p.m. Prezzo: dollari 5,50 a persona. Per i biglietti rivolgersi ai professori D'Aprano e Warren, tel. 81 0301, ex. 282, oppure a Frank Gonano, tel. 848 1522 (dalle 6,30 p.m. alle ore 11 p.m.)

**Sabato 8 giugno,** Serata danzante dei club italiani delle Università di Melbourne, Monash, La Trobe e dello Swimburne College, ai ritmi di due note orchestre. Prezzo di partecipazione: membri dollari 1,50; non membri dollari 2. La serata avrà inizio alle

## Fig and mascarpone pie
### *Torta ai fichi e mascarpone*

**Serves 8**

**Ingredients:**
100 g (3½ oz) digestive biscuits
    (graham crackers)
250 g (9 oz/1 cup) melted unsalted butter
1 kg (2 lb 3 oz/10 scoops) Mascarpone,
    berry and biscotti gelato (page 79)
10 whole figs, sliced
1 tablespoon caster (superfine) sugar
1 tablespoon aged balsamic vinegar
1 teaspoon vanilla paste
1 tablespoon water

*We do a mascarpone and fig flavoured gelato at the shop and this is like a cake version of that – biscuit shell on the bottom with a layer of mascarpone gelato and fresh sliced figs on the top. I love figs because they only arrive a couple of times a year and the season is so short they always seem rare and special.*

1    Place the biscuits in a large bowl and crush them with the end of a rolling pin to a fine crumb (alternatively, blitz them briefly to a similar consistency in a food processor). Pour the melted butter over the crushed biscuits and stir to combine.

2    Spoon the biscuit crumb mixture into a 20 cm (8 in) loose-bottomed pie tin and press it into the base and sides to cover evenly, being sure to leave no gaps. Transfer the pie shell to the freezer for 30 minutes to chill and firm.

3    Once chilled, spoon the gelato over the pie shell and spread it with a palette knife to form an even layer, then transfer to the freezer and leave to chill for 1 hour.

4    Meanwhile, add the figs, caster sugar, balsamic vinegar, vanilla paste and water to a bowl and mix to combine. Transfer to the fridge and leave to macerate for 10 minutes.

5    When ready to serve, remove the pie from the freezer, spoon over the macerated figs and juices evenly and slice into wedges.

**Makes 1 kg (2 lb 3 oz/10 scoops)**

**Ingredients:**
**600 g (1 lb 5 oz) freshly squeezed mandarin juice**
**200 g (7 oz) filtered water**
**2.5 g (⅛ oz) carob bean powder**
**200 g (7 oz) caster (superfine) sugar**

**Mandarin sorbetto**
***Sorbetto al mandarino***

*This is one of my favourite autumn flavours. I like to serve this on its own because mandarin is not a common flavour, so it's nice to just concentrate on it all on its own. It's so refreshing and works really well as a palate cleanser.*

1   Put the mandarin juice and water in a bowl and blend with a hand-held blender to combine.

2   Put the carob bean powder in a separate bowl. Add 2 tablespoons of the sugar and mix together well.

3   Gradually add the carob bean powder mixture to the mandarin mixture, blending all the while, until well combined. Add the rest of the sugar and blend to incorporate, then transfer to a suitable lidded container and leave to cool in the freezer for 1 hour, or until the mixture drops to 4°C (39°F).

4   Turn on your gelato maker so it begins the freezing process.

5   Pour the mixture into your gelato maker. Once the mixture reaches –4°C (25°F) (this should take about 30–40 minutes) detach the canister or scoop the sorbetto into a pre-cooled lidded container. Transfer to the freezer and leave for at least 1 hour to harden before serving.

**Popcorn choc top**
*Popcorn ricoperti di cioccolato*

**Makes 10**

**Ingredients:**
**10 good-quality waffle cones**

**Popcorn gelato**
**20 g (¾ oz) unsalted butter**
**100 g (3½ oz) popcorn kernels**
**135 g (5 oz) caster (superfine) sugar**
**35 g (1¼ oz) dextrose**
**20 g (¾ oz) skim milk powder**
**5 g (¼ oz) carob bean powder**
**645 g (1 lb 7 oz) milk**
**165 g (6 oz) pouring (single/light) cream**

**Chocolate topping**
**200 g (7 oz) dark chocolate**
**(60% cocoa solids)**
**80 g (2¾ oz) cocoa butter**

*Popcorn gelato was a flavour I first came across when I was in Italy. There they used a popcorn-flavoured powder but we make fresh popcorn with butter, blend it with the base mixture and then strain it to get all the bits out. Don't try and make your own cone – it's more trouble than it's worth and it won't be as good as the good-quality cones you can buy.*

1   For the popcorn gelato, melt the butter in a saucepan over a high heat. Add the popcorn kernels and shake to coat, then cover with a lid and shake a few more times until the popcorn starts popping. Once the popcorn stops popping, remove the pan from the heat and set aside.

2   Put the sugar, dextrose and skim milk powder in a bowl and mix to combine. Put the carob bean powder in a separate bowl, add 2 tablespoons of the sugar mixture and mix together well.

3   Pour the milk and cream into a large heavy-based saucepan over a medium heat. Whisk in the carob bean powder mixture and continue to heat, whisking in the sugar mixture as you go, until it hits 85°C (185°F).

4   Add the popcorn, setting aside a few handfuls for decoration. Remove from the heat and blend with a hand-held blender until as smooth as possible, then strain through a sieve. Pour into a suitable lidded container and leave to cool in the freezer for 1 hour, or until the mixture drops to 4°C (39°F).

5   Turn on your gelato maker so it begins the freezing process.

6   Pour the mixture into your gelato maker. Once the mixture reaches −4°C (25°F) or is the consistency of soft-serve ice cream (this should take about 30–45 minutes) detach the canister or scoop the gelato into a pre-cooled lidded container. Transfer to the freezer and leave for at least 1 hour to harden before serving.

7   To make the chocolate topping, add the chocolate and cocoa butter to a heatproof bowl set over a saucepan of boiling water and stir until melted. (Alternatively, place the bowl in the microwave and heat for 2 minutes.) Set the bowl aside on a work surface and leave to cool slightly for 2–3 minutes.

8   To assemble the choc tops, press a scoop of gelato into each cone, then invert it and dip it briefly in the melted chocolate mixture, ensuring the gelato is completely covered. Press the reserved popcorn into the melted chocolate to coat completely, if you like, then transfer the choc top to a stand in the freezer and repeat with the remaining choc tops. Leave the choc tops for at least 30 minutes to harden before eating.

140-

# 181

Anyone who doesn't believe that winter and gelato go together should have come to the closing night of our temporary store. We'd decided to celebrate the success of the store and preview the opening of the permanent Pidapipó in a few months' time by holding an event, like a closing night party. We called the event the Last Lick, organised a DJ and put it out there that we were giving away a free scoop to every customer. Luckily, I'd prepared enough to get us started. We usually make the gelato as we go but I thought because we were giving it away that we might be a bit busier than usual. We were. It was a freezing cold night in July and the line just kept getting longer and longer, stretching for blocks along Faraday Street, almost to Melbourne Uni.

It was an absolutely crazy night. I had to send Jamie down to the local supermarket a few times to bring back trolleys full of milk because we kept running out and at one stage I had the DJ helping me pour milk into the machine. It was unbelievable. I know that free gelato is a pretty good deal but all those people standing around outside in beanies, gloves, coats and scarves eating gelato showed me that it is something people want to snack on all year round. We might not be at the same level as Italy, where people go out for gelato like we go out for coffee, but we're on the way.

Winter obviously limits the kind of fruit you can source but some of the produce you do get at this time of year – blood oranges, pears, kiwi fruit, lemons and so on – is as good as any of the flavours you can get in summer. And then there's winter's chocolate factor. Chocolate and gelato is a popular combination all year round but it's a particular favourite when the weather gets colder.

The most popular flavour on our menu in winter, though, are the ones that feature Nutella. The idea of swirling Nutella through our gelato first came to me in the temporary store and kind of happened by accident. On this particular day I'd run out of certain ingredients and so I had to come up with something else to put on the menu. I had all this Nutella that was sitting around on the shelves, just for decoration really. We weren't using it at the time. I was thinking about stracciatella, which is one of the most popular Italian flavours, like chocolate chip in fior di latte. And then I thought, 'I wonder what would happen if I put Nutella instead of the chocolate chip in the fior di latte?' I didn't know if it would work but as soon as I tried it I knew it was great. Then I thought that it would be even better if we put the Nutella straight on top. We decided to try it that way and it straightaway became our most popular flavour. It was how our Nutella tap was born because from then on we had to have a constant flow of it in the shop.

Chocolate was also used in one of my favourite winter collaborations. I teamed up with Harry and Charlie, a pair of young chocolate-making brothers who work under the name

Hunted + Gathered. They make their chocolate from scratch, from beans they source ethically. They don't use cane sugar (they use coconut) or dairy (except when I wanted to do something with milk chocolate and so they agreed to custom make it for me) and their chocolate is all around 70 per cent cacao. It's dark and intense. The winter range we did with them was called Death By Chocolate and included three different gelati: dark chocolate fondant with candied orange, malted milk chocolate with caramel, and a chocolate gelato with salted chocolate ganache.

Winter is when we do some of our most interesting collaborations. The Melbourne International Film Festival approached us to do gelato in little cups that would be sold at all the cinemas playing their films. I did two flavours for that, popcorn and caramel, and a zabaglione and biscotti. Another collaboration was with chef Pierre Roelofs, who is famous for his multi-course dessert evenings that he holds at different venues. He'd been on the list of people I'd always wanted to work with so when he reached out to us it was a great compliment. We brainstormed some ideas and decided we would recreate one of his dessert nights at Pidapipó, pairing his desserts with our gelato. It was a ticketed event with two seatings of 15 people a night.

I can't imagine going without gelato during the winter. You just have to work out the right kind of gelato to eat. Believe me, there's plenty of choice.

**Pumpkin pie**
*Torta alla zucca*

Serves 8

Ingredients:

100 g (3½ oz) digestive biscuits
    (graham crackers)
250 g (9 oz/1 cup) unsalted butter, melted
1 kg (2 lb 3 oz/10 scoops) Spiced pumpkin
    gelato (page 150)

Caramel sauce

85 g (3 oz) soft brown sugar
85 ml (2¾ fl oz) pouring
    (single/light) cream
25 g (1 oz) unsalted butter

Pecan croccante

1 tablespoon glucose syrup
65 g (2¼ oz) caster (superfine) sugar
65 g (2¼ oz/⅔ cup) pecans

*Spiced pumpkin is one of my favourite winter flavours. We make spiced pumpkin gelato specifically for our pumpkin pie but we also sell it in cones because it's one of those flavours that some people really, really like. Once you've tried it, there's no going back.*

1    To make the caramel sauce, add the brown sugar and cream to a small heavy-based saucepan over a medium heat and, whisking, bring to the boil. Add the butter and cook, whisking continuously, until it has melted completely, then remove from the heat. Pour into a bowl, transfer to the fridge and leave to chill.

2    For the pecan croccante, add the glucose syrup and caster sugar to a small saucepan over a high heat. Cook, stirring, until caramelised and very dark brown in colour, then add the pecans and mix together thoroughly. Carefully tip the mixture out onto the centre of a heatproof silicone mat, cover with non-stick baking paper and roll out with a rolling pin as thin as possible. Leave to cool, then pull off the paper and chop into rough pieces. Set aside until needed.

3    Place the biscuits in a large bowl and crush them with the end of a rolling pin to a fine crumb (alternatively, blitz them briefly to a similar consistency in a food processor). Pour the melted butter over the crushed biscuits and stir to combine.

4    Spoon the biscuit mixture into a 20 cm (8 in) loose-bottomed pie tin and press it into the base and sides to cover evenly, being sure to leave no gaps. Transfer the pie shell to the freezer for 1 hour to chill and firm.

5    Once chilled, spoon the gelato over the pie shell and spread it with a palette knife to form an even layer, then transfer to the freezer and leave to chill for 1 hour.

6    When ready to serve, remove the pie from the freezer, pour over the caramel sauce and scatter over the pecan croccante.

Winter
*Inverno*

## Spiced pumpkin gelato
### *Gelato alla zucca speziata*

**Makes 1 kg (2 lb 3 oz/10 scoops)**

**Ingredients:**
375 g (13 oz) butternut pumpkin (squash),
   cut into rough chunks
80 g (2¾ oz) caster (superfine) sugar
50 g (1¾ oz) dextrose
10 g (¼ oz) skim milk powder
3 g (⅛ oz) carob bean powder
415 g (14½ oz) milk
100 ml (3½ fl oz) pouring
   (single/light) cream
½ teaspoon ground allspice
½ teaspoon ground cardamom

*We tend not to think of pumpkin as a dessert ingredient in Australia but it actually works really well. This is a great option for those who prefer more savoury flavours.*

1   Add the butternut pumpkin to a saucepan of boiling water and cook for 15–20 minutes until tender. Drain and set aside to cool.

2   Put the sugar, dextrose and skim milk powder in a bowl and mix to combine.

3   Put the carob bean powder in a separate bowl. Add 2 tablespoons of the sugar mixture and mix together well.

4   Add the milk, cream, allspice and cardamom to a large heavy-based saucepan over a medium heat. Whisk in the carob bean powder mixture and continue to heat, whisking in the sugar mixture as you go, until it hits 85°C (185°F).

5   Remove from the heat, add the pumpkin and blend with a hand-held blender until smooth, then pour into a suitable lidded container and leave to cool in the freezer for 1 hour, or until the mixture drops to 4°C (39°F).

6   Turn on your gelato maker so it begins the freezing process.

7   Pour the mixture into your gelato maker. Once the mixture reaches –4°C (25°F ) or is the consistency of soft-serve ice cream (this should take about 30–45 minutes) detach the canister or scoop the gelato into a pre-cooled lidded container. Transfer to the freezer and leave for at least 1 hour to harden before serving.

## Pistachio gelato
### *Gelato al pistacchio*

**Makes 1 kg (2 lb 3 oz/10 scoops)**

**Ingredients:**
**135 g (5 oz) caster (superfine) sugar**
**40 g (1½ oz) dextrose**
**20 g (¾ oz) skim milk powder**
**5 g (¼ oz) carob bean powder**
**645 g (1 lb 7 oz) milk**
**165 ml (5½ fl oz) pouring**
    **(single/light) cream**
**100 g (3½ oz) pistachio paste**

*Pistachio is the go-to gelato flavour in Italy, so it seems about right that it's one of our most popular flavours in our Carlton shop in the heart of Melbourne's Little Italy. In Italy they say that if you want to tell if it's a good gelateria you should taste the pistachio nuts. I use a pistachio paste to make this gelato, an Italian one from Bronte in Italy. A good-quality pistachio paste will never be bright green – that just shows that colours have been added and it's probably not the best flavour. Good pistachio paste will be a dark brown-green colour.*

1    Put the sugar, dextrose and skim milk powder in a bowl and mix to combine.

2    Put the carob bean powder in a separate bowl. Add 2 tablespoons of the sugar mixture and mix together well.

3    Pour the milk and cream into a large heavy-based saucepan over a medium heat. Whisk in the carob bean powder mixture and continue to heat, whisking in the sugar mixture as you go, until it hits 85°C (185°F).

4    Add the pistachio paste to the mixture and blend with a hand-held blender until smooth and combined. Remove from the heat, pour into a suitable lidded container and leave to cool in the freezer for 1 hour, or until the mixture drops to 4°C (39°F).

5    Turn on your gelato maker so it begins the freezing process.

6    Pour the mixture into your gelato maker. Once the mixture reaches −4°C (25°F ) or is the consistency of soft-serve ice cream (this should take about 30–45 minutes) detach the canister or scoop the gelato into a pre-cooled lidded container. Transfer to the freezer and leave for at least 1 hour to harden before serving.

## Brioche with pistachio gelato and whipped cream
### *Brioche con gelato al pistacchio e panna montata*

**Serves 5**

**Ingredients:**
250 ml (8½ fl oz/1 cup) pouring (single/light) cream
25 g (1 oz) icing (confectioners') sugar
500 g (1 lb 2 oz/5 scoops) Pistachio gelato (page 151)

**Brioche**
200 ml (7 fl oz) cold milk
2 teaspoons table salt
1 tablespoon honey
2¼ teaspoons dry yeast
500 g (1 lb 2 oz) 00 flour
75 g (2¾ oz) caster (superfine) sugar
2 eggs
75 g (2¾ oz) cold unsalted butter, cubed

**Egg wash**
1 egg
100 ml (3½ fl oz) milk

*I've put pistachio gelato with brioche here because I wanted to team a classic with a classic. The brioche recipe is the one we use in the shops for our gelato sandwiches. We got it from a pastry chef in Italy. It's time-consuming to make brioche because you need to let the dough prove but it's really rewarding once you've mastered it, and the results are light and fluffy.*

1    Line a baking tray with non-stick baking paper.

2    Place the pouring cream and icing sugar in a bowl and whisk with a hand whisk or electric hand whisk until soft peaks form. Transfer to the fridge until ready to use.

3    To make the brioche, divide the milk equally between two mugs. Add the salt and honey to one and the yeast to the other and stir each to combine.

4    Place the flour and sugar in the bowl of an electric mixer with the dough hook attachment added. Turn the mixer on low and add the eggs, one at a time, leaving a 1 minute interval between each. Continue to mix for a further 8 minutes, then add the salt and honey mixture. Mix for a further 2 minutes, then add the milk and yeast mixture. Continue to mix, adding a cube or two of the cold butter every few minutes, for 30 minutes, or until a smooth dough has formed that comes away from the sides of the bowl.

5    Transfer the dough to a mixing bowl, cover with plastic wrap and leave to rest in the fridge for 2 hours.

6    Once rested, remove the dough from the fridge and divide it out into five 90 g (3 oz) pieces and five 10 g (¼ oz) pieces. Roll each piece into a perfectly round ball, then arrange the bigger pieces on the baking tray lined with non-stick baking paper, leaving a gap of at least 2 cm (¾ in) between each piece.

7    Wet the tip of your index finger with water and gently push it into the centre of a larger dough piece to form a slight indentation. Place one of the smaller pieces on top of the indentation and press it down gently to stick the two pieces together (if they don't stick together, try again using a little more water). Repeat with the remaining dough pieces, then transfer the tray to a warm spot and leave to rise for 3 hours, or until tripled in size.

*Continues on following page*

8    Preheat the oven to 180°C (350°F/Gas 4). For the egg wash, whisk the egg and milk together in a small bowl until combined.

9    Once risen, use a pastry brush to lightly brush the brioche all over with the egg wash, then bake in the oven for 4 minutes. Remove the brioche from the oven and increase the heat to 200°C (400°F/Gas 6). Cover the brioche with aluminium foil and return to the oven for 10 minutes, until golden. Remove from the oven and leave to cool slightly on a wire rack.

10   To assemble, slice the still-warm brioche in half, place a scoop of the pistachio gelato on the base of each and top with a dollop of the whipped cream. Sandwich together with the remaining brioche halves and serve immediately.

TIP This works well with the brioche cold if you want to make them in advance, though if you prefer it hot you can always warm the pre-made brioche in the microwave for 45 seconds or so just before serving.

A PIANTA PROSPET
DI VICENZA DEI

## Tiramisu layer cake
### *Tiramisù a strati*

**Serves 6**

**Ingredients:**
**Mascarpone gelato**
120 g (4½ oz) caster (superfine) sugar
50 g (1¾ oz) dextrose
15 g (½ oz) skim milk powder
3 g (⅛ oz) carob bean powder
485 g (1 lb 1 oz) milk
125 ml (4 fl oz/½ cup) pouring
    (single/light) cream
25 g (1 oz) filtered water
25 g (1 oz) egg yolk
150 g (5½ oz) mascarpone

**Tiramisu layer cake**
500 ml (17 fl oz/2 cups) freshly brewed
    espresso coffee
500 ml (17 fl oz/2 cups) sweet sherry
200 g (7 oz) savoiardi (lady fingers)
100 g (3½ oz) dark chocolate
    (70% cocoa solids)

*I don't think I've ever met anyone who doesn't like tiramisu. This version is based on one of the concepts that I was taught at the gelato university in Bologna but it also reminds me of home because my mum has always made tiramisu. She's a tiramisu snob – she always orders it in restaurants and it's never good enough so the bar was set pretty high for me with this one. What makes my mum's tiramisu so good is that she soaks the savoiardi biscuits in coffee and sweet sherry. The sweet sherry is what makes it.*

1    To make the mascarpone gelato, put the sugar, dextrose and skim milk powder in a bowl and mix to combine. Put the carob bean powder in a separate bowl. Add 2 tablespoons of the sugar mixture and mix together well.

2    Add the milk, cream, water and egg yolk to a large heavy-based saucepan over a medium heat and whisk to combine. Whisk in the carob bean powder mixture and continue to heat, whisking in the sugar mixture as you go, until it hits 85°C (185°F).

3    Remove the pan from the heat, add the mascarpone and blend with a hand-held blender until smooth, then pour into a suitable lidded container and leave to cool in the freezer for 1 hour, or until the mixture drops to 4°C (39°F). Turn on your gelato maker so it begins the freezing process.

5    Pour the mixture into your gelato maker. Once the mixture reaches –4°C (25°F) or is the consistency of soft-serve ice cream (this should take about 30–45 minutes) detach the canister or scoop the gelato into a pre-cooled lidded container. Place the gelato in a freezer for 30 minutes to harden further.

6    To make the tiramisu layer cake, pour the freshly brewed coffee into a bowl together with the sherry and leave to chill for 1 hour, or until the mixture drops to 4°C (39°F).

7    Place 6 scoops of gelato onto a pre-cooled 29 × 20 cm (11½ × 8 in) shallow glass tray and spread it with a palette knife to form an even layer.

8    Place the chilled coffee and sherry mixture in a shallow bowl. Submerge the savoiardi biscuits briefly in the liquid, then layer them side by side on top of the gelato to cover completely, being careful not to leave any gaps.

9    Grate a layer of chocolate over the biscuits. Repeat the layers again, adding scoops of the remaining gelato on top to finish. If you like, use a spoon to mess up the top layer of gelato to make peaks, then transfer to the freezer and leave for at least 1 hour to harden.

10    When ready to serve, remove from the freezer and grate over a final layer of chocolate to finish, if you like.

**Chocolate fondant cake with fior d'arancia gelato**
*Torta al cioccolato fondente con gelato al fior d'arancio*

**Serves 5**

**Ingredients:**

160 g (5½ oz) dark chocolate
    (70% cocoa solids)
160 g (5½ oz/⅔ cup) unsalted butter, plus
    extra for greasing
3 eggs
3 egg yolks
½ teaspoon vanilla paste
85 g (3 oz) caster (superfine) sugar
45 g (1½ oz) plain (all-purpose) flour
icing (confectioners') sugar, for dusting

**Fior d'arancia gelato**
135 g (5 oz) caster (superfine) sugar
35 g (1¼ oz) dextrose
20 g (¾ oz) skim milk powder
5 g (¼ oz) carob bean powder
zest of 2 oranges
645 g (1 lb 7 oz) milk
165 ml (5½ fl oz) pouring
    (single/light) cream

*Chocolate fondant cake is like a self-saucing pudding, gooey and delicious. If you cook it correctly – pay careful attention to the cooking times to guarantee a properly soft centre – it's the best thing ever. The gelato is made from fior di latte mixed with orange zest, a clean flavour that works beautifully with the chocolate.*

1    For the fior d'arancia gelato, put the sugar, dextrose and skim milk powder in a bowl and mix to combine.

2    Put the carob bean powder in a separate bowl. Add 2 tablespoons of the sugar mixture and mix together well.

3    Add the orange zest, milk and cream to a large heavy-based saucepan over a medium heat. Whisk in the carob bean powder mixture and continue to heat, whisking in the sugar mixture as you go, until it hits 85°C (185°F). Remove from the heat, pour into a suitable lidded container and leave to cool in the freezer for 1 hour, or until the mixture drops to 4°C (39°F).

4    Turn on your gelato maker so it begins the freezing process.

5    Pour the mixture into your gelato maker. Once the mixture reaches –4°C (25°F ) or is the consistency of soft-serve ice cream (this should take about 30–45 minutes) detach the canister or scoop the gelato into a pre-cooled lidded container. Transfer to the freezer and leave for at least 1 hour to harden.

6    Preheat the oven to 190°C (375°F/Gas 5). Grease five 50 ml (1¾ fl oz) ramekins with a little butter.

7    Melt the chocolate and butter together in a double boiler. Remove from the heat and leave to cool slightly.

8    Whisk the eggs, egg yolks, vanilla and sugar together in a bowl until pale and fluffy. Sift over the flour and fold everything together, then add the chocolate and butter mixture and fold to combine. Pour the mixture into the prepared ramekins, transfer to the oven and bake for 12 minutes, or until the surface of the fondants is cooked but still soft to the touch.

9    Remove the ramekins from the oven and turn the fondants out onto serving plates. To serve, dust the fondants with a little icing sugar and serve alongside a scoop of fior d'arancia gelato. Eat straight away.

## Vanilla rice pudding with cardamom and pistachio gelato and butterscotch sauce
### *Budino di riso alla vaniglia con gelato al pistacchio, cardamomo e crema toffee*

**Serves 4 with extra gelato**

**Ingredients:**
200 g (7 oz) arborio rice
1.25 litres (42 fl oz/5 cups) milk, plus
    extra if necessary
125 ml (4 fl oz/½ cup) pouring
    (single/light) cream
110 g (4 oz) caster (superfine) sugar
1 vanilla bean, split lengthways and
    seeds scraped
pinch of freshly ground nutmeg
150 g (5½ oz) crushed pistachio nuts

**Cardamom and pistachio gelato**
135 g (5 oz) caster (superfine) sugar
35 g (1¼ oz) dextrose
20 g (¾ oz) skim milk powder
20 g (¾ oz) freshly ground cardamom
5 g (¼ oz) carob bean powder
645 g (1 lb 7 oz) milk
315 ml (10½ fl oz) pouring
    (single/light) cream
100 g (3½ oz) condensed milk
100 g (3½ oz) crushed pistachio nuts

**Butterscotch sauce**
155 g (5½ oz) soft brown sugar
160 ml (5½ fl oz) pouring
    (single/light) cream
50 g (1¾ oz) unsalted butter

*This recipe pays homage to my sister Amanda, who loves rice pudding more than any other dessert. To make things a bit more interesting I've paired the rice pudding with a warm butterscotch sauce that goes brilliantly with the nuts and spices in the gelato, which was inspired by the Indian dessert kulfi. A comforting dessert whatever the time of year.*

1    For the gelato, put the sugar, dextrose, skim milk powder and ground cardamom in a bowl and mix to combine.

2    Put the carob bean powder in a separate bowl. Add 2 tablespoons of the sugar mixture and mix together well.

3    Pour the milk and cream into a large heavy-based saucepan over a medium heat. Whisk in the carob bean powder mixture and continue to heat, whisking in the sugar mixture as you go, until it hits 85°C (185°F).

4    Remove from the heat, pour into a suitable lidded container and leave to cool in the freezer for 1 hour, or until the mixture drops to 4°C (39°F). Add the condensed milk and blend with a hand-held blender until combined.

5    Turn on your gelato maker so it begins the freezing process.

6    Pour the mixture into your gelato maker. Once the mixture reaches −4°C (25°F ) or is the consistency of soft-serve ice cream (this should take about 30–45 minutes), mix in the crushed pistachio nuts evenly, then detach the canister or scoop the gelato into a pre-cooled lidded container. Transfer to the freezer and leave for 1 hour to harden.

7    Add the rice, milk, cream, sugar, vanilla seeds and nutmeg to a heavy-based saucepan over a high heat and bring to the boil. Reduce the heat to low and cook, stirring every few minutes, for 30 minutes, or until the rice is soft, adding more milk if the rice pudding looks like it is getting too thick.

8    Meanwhile, make the butterscotch sauce. Whisk the sugar and cream together in a small heavy-based saucepan over a medium heat. Bring to the boil, add the butter and cook, whisking continuously, until it has melted completely. Keep warm.

9    To serve, divide the rice pudding among 4 bowls, spoon over the butterscotch sauce, sprinkle over the crushed pistachios and top each bowl with a scoop of the cardamom and pistachio gelato.

Winter
*Inverno*

**Zabaglione gelato**
*Gelato allo zabaglione*

**Makes 1 kg (2 lb 3 oz/10 scoops)**

**Ingredients:**
80 g (2¾ oz) caster (superfine) sugar
20 g (¾ oz) dextrose
10 g (¼ oz) skim milk powder
2½ g (⅛ oz) carob bean powder
385 g (13½ oz) milk
195 ml (6½ fl oz) pouring
            (single/light) cream

**Zabaglione sauce**
120 ml (4 fl oz) marsala
90 g (3 oz) egg yolks
90 g (3 oz) caster (superfine) sugar

*Not everybody knows what zabaglione is but they should do, because it's delicious! The people who do know about it can't get enough. It's rich and creamy and is flavoured with marsala, kind of like a vanilla ice cream on steroids.*

1   To make the zabaglione sauce, add all the sauce ingredients to a heatproof bowl set over a saucepan of lightly simmering water. Whisk continuously until the mixture is foamy and thick enough to coat the back of a spoon (be careful not to overcook it – you don't want scrambled egg here!). Remove from the heat and set aside to cool.

2   Put the sugar, dextrose and skim milk powder in a bowl and mix to combine.

3   Put the carob bean powder in a separate bowl. Add 2 tablespoons of the sugar mixture and mix together well.

4   Pour the milk and cream into a large heavy-based saucepan over a medium heat. Whisk in the carob bean powder mixture and continue to heat, whisking in the sugar mixture as you go, until it hits 85°C (185°F).

5   Remove from the heat, add the zabaglione sauce and blend with a hand-held blender to combine, then pour into a suitable lidded container and leave to cool in the freezer for 1 hour, or until the mixture drops to 4°C (39°F).

6   Turn on your gelato maker so it begins the freezing process.

7   Pour the mixture into your gelato maker. Once the mixture reaches –4°C (25°F ) or is the consistency of soft-serve ice cream (this should take about 30–45 minutes) detach the canister or scoop the gelato into a pre-cooled lidded container. Transfer to the freezer and leave for at least 1 hour to harden before serving.

**Zabaglione, zabaglione gelato with savoiardi biscuits**
*Gelato allo zabaglione con biscotti savoiardi*

**Serves 4**

**Ingredients:**
4 savoiardi biscuits (lady fingers)
400 g (14 oz/4 scoops) Zabaglione gelato
    (page 163)

**Zabaglione sauce**
240 g (8½ oz) marsala
180 g (6½ oz) egg yolks
180 g (6½ oz) caster (superfine) sugar

*This is a really simple recipe and it works well in winter because it's so heavy and rich. It's based on a traditional Italian dessert and while there are only three key ingredients, the technique behind it can be a bit difficult. You don't want to cook zabaglione too long because you'll scramble the eggs but you have to heat it enough so that you've cooked the eggs to the proper thick and creamy consistency. You can serve the sauce cold but it's better if you serve it while it's still warm. Hot sauce, cold gelato, crunchy biscuits – it has it all!*

1    To make the zabaglione sauce, add all the ingredients to a heatproof bowl set over a saucepan of lightly simmering water. Whisk continuously until the mixture is foamy and thick enough to coat the back of a spoon (be careful not to overcook it – you don't want scrambled egg here!).

2    To assemble, crumble up the savoiardi biscuits and divide among bowls. Top each with a scoop of zabaglione gelato and pour the warm zabaglione sauce around the outside of the bowls. Serve.

**Ricotta filled cannoli**

*Cannoli ripieni di ricotta*

Makes approx. 50 cannoli

Ingredients:

Cannoli

250 g (9 oz/1⅔ cups) plain
    (all-purpose) flour

1 tablespoon caster (superfine) sugar

1 egg, separated

25 g (1 oz) softened butter

125 ml (4 fl oz/½ cup) sweet sherry, plus
    extra if necessary

vegetable oil, for deep-frying

Cassata gelato

105 g (3½ oz) caster (superfine) sugar

25 g (1 oz) dextrose

15 g (½ oz) skim milk powder

4 g (¼ oz) carob bean powder

500 g (1 lb 2 oz) milk

125 ml (4 fl oz/½ cup) pouring
    (single/light) cream

220 g (8 oz) cow's milk ricotta

100 g (3½ oz) candied cedro lemon,
    finely diced, plus extra to decorate

100 g (3½ oz) candied orange, finely
    diced, plus extra to decorate

*The recipe for the pastry cannoli shell here comes from a friend of mine whose family is Sicilian. You can make the shells in large quantities and then store them in the fridge until you're ready to pipe them with the ricotta-based gelato (it's best not to assemble them until you need them as they can get soggy if made up in advance and kept in the freezer). I've used traditional southern Italian cassata flavours – candied fruits and nuts and so on – in the gelato. If you can't be bothered making the shells, you should be able to get them from an Italian pastry shop.*

1    To make the cannoli, add the flour and sugar to the bowl of an electric mixer. Beat together on a low speed, adding the egg yolk, butter and sherry as you go, to form a soft dough, adding a little more sherry if the dough is too firm.

2    Roll the dough out through a pasta machine, one setting at a time, down to the second thinnest setting, then cut the dough sheets out into discs using a 10 cm (4 in) round cookie cutter.

3    Wrap the dough discs around 12 × 2.5 cm (5 × 1 in) metal cannoli tubes and brush with a little egg white to seal the sides together.

4    Fill a large saucepan half full with vegetable oil and heat to 170°C (340°F). Carefully lower the cannoli into the hot oil in batches and cook for 1–2 minutes until golden. Remove from the oil and drain on paper towel, then carefully slide the metal tubes out of one end and leave the shells seam-side down to cool completely. Store in a suitable container in the refrigerator until needed.

5    For the cassata gelato, put the sugar, dextrose and skim milk powder in a bowl and mix to combine.

6    Put the carob bean powder in a separate bowl. Add 2 tablespoons of the sugar mixture and mix together well.

7    Pour the milk and cream into a large heavy-based saucepan over a medium heat. Whisk in the carob bean powder mixture and continue to heat, whisking in the sugar mixture as you go, until it hits 85°C (185°F).

*Continues on following page*

8    Take the mixture off the heat, add the ricotta and blend with
     a hand-held blender until smooth, then pour into a suitable
     lidded container and leave to cool in the freezer for 1 hour, or
     until the mixture drops to 4°C (39°F).

9    Turn on your gelato maker so it begins the freezing process.

10   Pour the mixture into your gelato maker. Once the mixture
     reaches −4°C (25°F) or is the consistency of soft-serve ice cream
     (this should take about 30–45 minutes) detach the canister or
     scoop the gelato into a pre-cooled lidded container. Transfer
     to the freezer and leave for at least 1 hour to harden.

11   Remove the gelato from the freezer, add the diced candied fruit
     and stir to combine, then transfer back to the freezer and leave
     for another hour to harden further.

12   To assemble the cannoli, fill a piping bag with the cassata gelato
     and pipe each side of the cannoli shell with the gelato (if the
     gelato is too hard to pipe easily, put it in the bowl of an electric
     mixer with the paddle attachment added and beat it briefly to
     soften). Dip the ends of each cannoli in more candied lemon
     and orange, and eat right away.

## Panettone bread and butter pudding with ginger gelato
### *Panettone e budino al burro con gelato allo zenzero*

*Bread and butter pudding is my dad's favourite dessert, so I knew I had to include a recipe for it here. I like to use panettone rather than brioche because of all the extra flavours it brings to the party – the candied fruit and so on – which help to make it special. This also makes it a really good dessert to serve at Christmas when you often have panettone left over. It's homely, simple and it makes everybody – especially my dad – happy.*

**Serves 8**

Ingredients:
butter, for greasing
500 ml (17 fl oz/2 cups) milk
500 ml (17 fl oz/2 cups) pouring
    (single/light) cream
4 eggs
1 tablespoon vanilla paste
115 g (4 oz/½ cup) caster (superfine)
    sugar
1 × 750 g (1 lb 11 oz) panettone, cut
    into wedges

Ginger gelato
135 g (5 oz) caster (superfine) sugar
35 g (1¼ oz) dextrose
20 g (¾ oz) skim milk powder
5 g (¼ oz) carob bean powder
645 g (1 lb 7 oz) milk
165 ml (5½ fl oz) pouring
    (single/light) cream
4 tablespoons freshly grated ginger

1    For the ginger gelato, put the sugar, dextrose and skim milk powder in a bowl and mix to combine.

2    Put the carob bean powder in a separate bowl. Add 2 tablespoons of the sugar mixture and mix together well.

3    Pour the milk and cream into a large heavy-based saucepan over a medium heat. Whisk in the carob bean powder mixture and continue to heat, whisking in the sugar mixture as you go, until it hits 85°C (185°F). Remove from the heat, pour into a suitable lidded container and leave to cool in the freezer for 1 hour, or until the mixture drops to 4°C (39°F).

4    Turn on your gelato maker so it begins the freezing process.

5    Add the ginger to the mixture and blend with a hand-held blender until smooth.

6    Pour the mixture into your gelato maker. Once the mixture reaches –4°C (25°F) or is the consistency of soft-serve ice cream (this should take about 30–45 minutes) detach the canister or scoop the gelato into a pre-cooled lidded container. Transfer to the freezer and leave for at least 1 hour to harden before serving.

7    To make the bread and butter pudding, preheat the oven to 170°C (340°F/Gas 3) and lightly grease a 35 × 25 cm (14 × 10 in) ovenproof dish with a little butter.

8    Whisk the milk, cream, eggs, vanilla paste and caster sugar together in a bowl until combined. Dip the panettone wedges briefly in the liquid mixture to coat, then arrange in the prepared baking dish in an even layer. Pour over the remaining mixture, place the dish in a roasting tray and pour enough boiling water into the tray to come halfway up the sides of the dish. Bake for 45 minutes until the custard has just set and the pudding is lightly golden.

9    Divide the pudding among bowls and serve with scoops of the ginger gelato.

## Hazelnut and Nutella gelato with biscotti crumble
### *Gelato alle nocciole e nutella con biscotti sbriciolati*

**Makes 1 kg (2 lb 3 oz/10 scoops)**

**Ingredients:**
135 g (5 oz) caster (superfine) sugar
45 g (1½ oz) dextrose
20 g (¾ oz) skim milk powder
5 g (¼ oz) carob bean powder
645 g (1 lb 7 oz) milk
165 ml (5½ fl oz) pouring
    (single/light) cream
100 g (3½ oz) hazelnut paste
80 g (2¾ oz) Nutella

**Hazelnut biscotti**
6 egg whites
450 g (1 lb) caster (superfine) sugar
2 vanilla beans, split lengthways and
    seeds scraped
2 teaspoons ground cinnamon
450 g (1 lb) roasted hazelnuts, crushed

*For this flavour I collaborated with an Italian restaurant in Melbourne called Baby. The head chef, Nicola Totaro, provided the biscotti recipe. They would also cook the hazelnut biscotti in the kitchen at Baby and then I would go and pick it up and use it in our gelato. The biscotti is amazing, with an almost meringue-like texture.*

1    Preheat the oven to 155°C (310°F/Gas 2). Line a baking tray with baking paper.

2    For the hazelnut biscotti, beat the egg whites and sugar together in the bowl of an electric mixer with the whisk attachment to form fluffy, firm peaks. Add the vanilla, cinnamon and crushed hazelnuts and mix everything together with a spoon, then pour into a heavy-based saucepan over a medium heat and heat to 80°C (175°F).

3    Remove the pan from the heat and spread the mixture over the baking tray in an even layer. Bake for 30 minutes, or until the biscuit is completely dry. Leave on a wire rack to cool, then chop into rough pieces. Set aside.

4    Put the sugar, dextrose and skim milk powder in a bowl and mix to combine.

5    Put the carob bean powder in a separate bowl. Add 2 tablespoons of the sugar mixture and mix together well.

6    Pour the milk and cream into a large heavy-based saucepan over a medium heat. Whisk in the carob bean powder mixture and continue to heat, whisking in the sugar mixture as you go, until it hits 85°C (185°F).

7    Remove from the heat, add the hazelnut paste and blend with a hand-held blender until combined and smooth. Pour into a suitable lidded container and leave to cool in the freezer for 1 hour, or until the mixture drops to 4°C (39°F).

8    Turn on your gelato maker so it begins the freezing process.

9    Pour the mixture into your gelato maker. Once the mixture reaches –4°C (25°F ) or is the consistency of soft-serve ice cream (this should take about 30–45 minutes) detach the canister or scoop the gelato into a pre-cooled lidded container. Transfer to the freezer and leave for 1 hour to harden.

10    Heat the Nutella in a double boiler or microwave until runny. Remove the Nutella from the heat and leave it to cool to room temperature, then add it to the gelato, drizzling it over and mixing it in with a spatula to break it up into a chip. Mix through the biscotti crumbs, then return the gelato to the freezer and leave for at least 1 hour to harden before serving.

**Kiwi sorbetto**

*Sorbetto al kiwi*

**Makes 1 kg (2 lb 3 oz/10 scoops)**

**Ingredients:**
**400 g (14 oz) kiwi flesh**
**380 g (13½ oz) filtered water**
**2.5 g (⅛ oz) carob bean powder**
**220 g (8 oz) caster (superfine) sugar**

*This is one of the key winter flavours at Pidapipó – a lot of other fruits appear a couple of times during the year but with kiwi fruit, it's only winter. It's such a strong flavour and it's also acidic, so it's really refreshing. It's also a dense-textured fruit, which makes for a really creamy textured sorbetto.*

1   Put the kiwi flesh and water in a bowl and blend with a hand-held blender until smooth.

2   Put the carob bean powder in a separate bowl. Add 2 tablespoons of the sugar and mix together well.

3   Gradually add the carob bean powder mixture to the kiwi mixture, blending all the while, until well combined. Add the rest of the sugar and blend to incorporate, then transfer to a suitable lidded container and leave to cool in the freezer for 30 minutes, or until the mixture drops to 4°C (39°F).

4   Turn on your gelato maker so it begins the freezing process.

5   Pour the mixture into your gelato maker. Once the mixture reaches –4°C (25°F) (this should take about 30–40 minutes) detach the canister or scoop the sorbetto into a pre-cooled lidded container. Transfer to the freezer and leave for at least 1 hour to harden before serving.

Winter
*Inverno*

**Grapefruit granita**
*Granita al pompelmo*

Serves 4

Ingredients:
600 g (1 lb 5 oz) freshly squeezed
        grapefruit juice
200 g (7 oz) filtered water
200 g (7 oz) caster (superfine) sugar

*Citrus fruits are commonly used in granita and grapefruit is one of my favourites because it has that slightly bitter taste that I really like. It's never too sweet. We use ruby grapefruit in our gelato but you can use any of kind of grapefruit really. Rubys are sweeter and I like the colour as well. This is another good granita for mixing with alcohol to make into a refreshing pre-dinner drink.*

1    Add the grapefruit juice, water and sugar to a bowl and blend with a hand-held blender until the sugar has dissolved.

2    Pour the mixture into a pre-cooled stainless steel tray and put into the freezer. Every 30 minutes, remove and break up the ice crystals with a fork. Do this until icy and easy to scoop (this should take about 2 hours). Serve.

### Blood orange granita with dark chocolate sorbetto
*Granita all'arancia sanguinella con sorbetto al cioccolato fondente*

**Serves 4**

**Ingredients:**

**Dark chocolate sorbetto**
85 g (3 oz) caster (superfine) sugar
3 g (1/8 oz) carob bean powder
20 g (¾ oz) Dutch (unsweetened)
    cocoa powder
290 g (10 oz) filtered water
100 g (3½ oz) dark chocolate (70% cocoa
    solids), broken into small chunks

**Blood orange granita**
600 g (1 lb 5 oz) freshly squeezed blood
    orange juice
200 g (7 oz) filtered water
200 g (7 oz) caster (superfine) sugar

*Chocolate sorbet is one of the most time-consuming flavours to make and one of our most popular – particularly among vegans (we use a chocolate that's dairy-free). This sorbetto is really rich and because there's no milk you really taste the chocolate. The blood orange granita here goes brilliantly with the chocolate but it's pretty good on its own too.*

1   For the dark chocolate sorbetto, put the caster sugar, carob bean powder and cocoa powder in a bowl and mix together to combine.

2   Pour the water into a heavy-based saucepan set over a medium heat. Gradually whisk in the sugar mixture and continue to heat until it hits 85°C (185°F). Remove from the heat, add the chocolate and whisk together until the chocolate has melted into the mixture and everything is well combined. Pour into a suitable lidded container and leave to cool in the freezer for 1 hour, or until the mixture drops to 4°C (39°F).

3   Turn on your gelato maker so it begins the freezing process.

4   Pour the chocolate sorbetto mixture into your gelato maker. Once the mixture reaches –4°C (25°F) or is the consistency of soft-serve ice cream (this should take about 30–45 minutes) detach the canister or scoop the sorbetto into a pre-cooled lidded container. Transfer to the freezer and leave for at least 1 hour to harden before serving.

5   For the granita, add the blood orange juice, water and sugar to a bowl and blend with a hand-held blender until the sugar has dissolved.

6   Pour the mixture into a pre-cooled stainless steel tray and put into the freezer. Every 30 minutes, remove and break up the ice crystals with a fork. Do this until icy and easy to scoop (this should take about 2 hours).

7   To serve, divide the granita among glasses and top each with a scoop of the dark chocolate sorbetto.

# Didapipó MILK BASED Flavour

| | | | |
|---|---|---|---|
| Nutella Swirl | Hazelnut | Salted Caramel | Fior di Latte |
| Cinnamon and Raisin | Chocolate | Bacio | Zabaio |
| Pistacchio | Banana MILK | Coconut | Mix Ber w Choc Ch |

Peanut Butter + Choc caramel • Pop Corn • MINT & White Ch Ri

| | | | |
|---|---|---|---|
| DAIRY FREE: | Watermelon | Mandarin | Pear |
| | Mango | | Lemo |

## About the Author

Lisa Valmorbida became obsessed with gelato slowly but emphatically. After leaving school she studied interior design but realised it was a career in food she craved. She studied and worked as a chef for a couple of years, ending up in a restaurant with a gelato machine in the kitchen. It was love at first sight. She enrolled in Bologna's acclaimed Carpigiani Gelato University, and followed with stints working in some of Italy's most renowned gelaterias. Back in Australia Lisa and her brother, Jamie, opened an Italian-style artisanal gelataria of their own. They named it Pidapipó, after a game they played with their nonno. There are now two Pidapipós in Melbourne, popular reflections of Lisa's delicious obsession.

## Acknowledgements

A big thanks to the publishing team at Hardie Grant, in particular Jane and Andrea, for pursuing and then persevering with this project and having the flexibility and patience to create a book in an unconventional way. It was a true collaboration and I couldn't have done it without you.

To the graphic designers at Fabio Ongarato Design, in particular Fabio, Ronnen, Tal and Jemma, thanks for your creative vision, design brilliance and being the awesome professionals you are who always have conviction in your work and care as much about the outcome as I do. It's better than I could have imagined.

Thanks to Michael Harden for being the ultimate gentleman and the very best wordsmith out there. I am very grateful and lucky to have collaborated with you on this book. Thank you to Simon Davis, the editor, who helped craft my text.

Thank you to the photography team, Lauren and Deb, for being so awesome and sticking out a very tough week on the job. You both could not have been more patient and professional.

To Jean Jullien, working on a project from the other side of the world can't have been easy but you grasped the brief from the beginning and approached it with rigour and creativity.

To our interior designer Rabindra Naidoo, I am so grateful for your unique vision and thoroughly designed spaces. You've designed each of our stores with the same enthusiasm and creativity and they just get better with age.

To the Pidapipó staff, thank you for being so good at what you do and allowing me the time and space I needed to write this book over many, many months.

To our many friends, suppliers, collaborators and customers, thank you for being a part of this special business. We are forever grateful for your ongoing support and partnership.

Big thanks also to mum and dad for putting up with me during the writing of this cookbook and for being so curious and patient throughout every rewrite of every recipe. And you thought I'd never finish!

And lastly to my brother and business partner, Jamie, who rarely gets a mention but has had my back from the start. If there's one person who cares more about the business than I do, it's him. I couldn't do what I do without him. And the best thing? The journey is only just beginning.

Published in 2017 by Hardie Grant Books, an imprint of Hardie Grant Publishing

Hardie Grant Books (Melbourne)
Building 1, 658 Church Street
Richmond, Victoria 3121

Hardie Grant Books (London)
5th & 6th floors
52–54 Southwark Street
London SE1 1UN

hardiegrantbooks.com

A Cataloguing-in-Publication entry is available from the catalogue of the
National Library of Australia at www.nla.gov.au

Pidapipó
ISBN 978 1 74379 336 7

Publishing Director: Jane Willson
Managing Editor: Marg Bowman
Project Editor: Andrea O'Connor
Editor: Simon Davis
Design Manager: Jessica Lowe
Designer: Fabio Ongarato Design
Illustrator: Jean Jullien
Photographers: Lauren Bamford, Jesper Hede
Stylist: Deb Kaloper
Production Manager: Todd Rechner

Colour reproduction by Splitting Image Colour Studio
Printed in China by 1010 Printing International Limited